"The power of positively spo[ken words impacts] children and adults. Ted McI[lvain illustrates] and guides us on how to hel[p build con]fidence, build positive self-wo[rth, especially as] related to public speaking. Ted punctuates his great message with fun activities that will bless all who are seeking to enjoy life more fully."

T. Charles Pierson
Chief Executive Officer of Big Brothers Big Sisters of North Texas

"An innovative approach to building tomorrow's leaders—teaching parents how to instill love, not fear, of public speaking. McIlvain has included the what, the why, and the how for parents and teachers who want to give their child a head start as a leader by becoming an effective communicator."

Dianna Booher
Author of *Communicate with Confidence* & *Speak with Confidence*

"Ted McIlvain graphically illustrates how and why, for better or for worse, people never get over what happen to them in the first six years of life. He makes practical application of profound psychological insights. A generous sprinkling of relevant anecdotal material makes it a very readable book. This is a "must-read" for parents and teachers of children under seven years of age."

Dr. Thomas Lane Butts
Pastor Emeritus of First United Methodist Church,
Monroeville, Alabama
Counselor, Newspaper Columnist, Nationally known preacher
Author of *Tigers in the Dark: A call to Courage and Christian Maturity*

"*Playground to Podium* is filled with relevant and engaging examples of subtle parental communication behaviors that have the power to influence a child's self-image, communication confidence, and success. I sincerely encourage all parents to take a little time in their busy lives to self-examine on the critical parent-child communication issues that Ted McIlvain brings to the surface."

Burt Pryor
Professor and Graduate Program Director
University of Central Florida Nicholson School of Communication

"If you want your children to develop confidence and positive self esteem, then *Playground to Podium* is for you. In his fun and up-beat style, Ted McIlvain outlines specific exercises that encourage your child's independence and growth. His 'training that strengthens' will help you be a more effective parent."

Bryan Flanagan
Flanagan Training
Group Father of Two
Author of *Now Go Sell Somebody Something*

"If parents wanted to offer a gift of self-confidence to their children, then they need look no further than Ted McIlvain's book *Playground to Podium*. This relatively small book has big ideas on how to instill confidence and self-assurance in children."

David Mosser
Professor, Public Speaker, Pastor
Author of *First Fruits: 14 Sermons on Stewardship*

"I was fortunate to have had Ted McIlvain as a professor before my first child reached the age of one. McIlvain's ideas about how to help your children become capable and confident communicators have changed the way my children are being raised. Story time is now one of my family's favorite times."

Travis Rall
TCU Student and Parent

"Bravo to Ted McIlvain for understanding you are never too young to develop those skills, and for equipping parents and teachers with not only theoretical knowledge, but also practical applications for hands-on, everyday training. Through vivid illustrations and poignant stories, Ted shows how very critical our interactions with children are, and the impact we have on shaping their lives. He also understands that when it comes to communication, only practice promotes proficiency. As a result, his activities are priceless!"

Robert Barnhill
Professional Speaker/Author
L.I.V.E. Speakers, Inc.
Past President, Toastmasters, International
Jana Barnhill
L.I.V.E. Speakers, Inc.
Second Vice President, Toastmasters, International

From Playground to Podium

Building Confidence for Public Speaking...A Parent's Guide

From Playground to Podium

Building Confidence for Public Speaking...A Parent's Guide

Ted McIlvain

TATE PUBLISHING & *Enterprises*

From Playground to Podium: Building Confidence for Speaking…A Parent's Guide
Copyright © 2007 by Ted McIlvain. All rights reserved.

This title is also available as a Tate Out Loud product. Visit www.tatepublishing.com for more information.

No part of this publication may be reproduced, stored in a retrieval system or transmitted in any way by any means, electronic, mechanical, photocopy, recording or otherwise without the prior permission of the author except as provided by USA copyright law.

This book is designed to provide accurate and authoritative information with regard to the subject matter covered. This information is given with the understanding that neither the author nor Tate Publishing, LLC is engaged in rendering legal, professional advice. Since the details of your situation are fact dependent, you should additionally seek the services of a competent professional.

The opinions expressed by the author are not necessarily those of Tate Publishing, LLC.

Published by Tate Publishing & Enterprises, LLC
127 E. Trade Center Terrace | Mustang, Oklahoma 73064 USA
1.888.361.9473 | www.tatepublishing.com

Tate Publishing is committed to excellence in the publishing industry. The company reflects the philosophy established by the founders, based on Psalms 68:11,
"The Lord gave the word and great was the company of those who published it."

Book design copyright © 2007 by Tate Publishing, LLC. All rights reserved.
Cover design by Jennifer L. Redden
Interior design by Lindsay B. Behrens

Published in the United States of America

ISBN: 978-1-60247-468-0
10.05.11

Dedication

For my family—Sandy, Brent, Kevin, Kerri, Lisa, and grandchildren—Abigail Sierra, Hannah Kate, Philip Alexander, Owen Lynn, Lily Ann and Grace Riley

Acknowledgments

I was fortunate to have studied with Dr. Burt Pryor at University of Central Florida, who first introduced me to the science of interpersonal communication and the art of public speaking. Dr. Ralph Behnke at Texas Christian University, who was my faculty advisor for the Masters program, believed I had the right stuff for being a teacher, professional speaker, and leader. I am grateful to both of these great research theorists and teachers in Communication Studies.

People who have influenced me to move this project forward:

Dianne, the first to suggest I write. EJay and Bill, my brothers, who believe I can write. TCU students who were willing to share their fears and show their courage in the classroom. Toastmasters International friends and colleagues who supported my competitive desires and helped me achieve TI's Accredited Speaker designation. Bertie and Tommie are parents who encouraged me to take the wheel early in life and never stop driving toward my goals.

Sandy, my wife, whose patience I challenged and from her support and courage I drew strength.

Contents

Introduction 15
Myths about Public Speaking 19
Costs of Gaining a Competitive Edge 27
Imagination Puts Your Stars in a Row 31
The Positive Approach to Discipline 39
Expectations and Trust. 43
Honesty Nurtures Relationships 51
Family Games Enhance Self-Esteem. 59
The Influence of Language Styles 65
Learn to Salvage Listening Errors 71
Making the Most of Storytelling. 75
Combating Negatives 83
Letting Go 87
Quality Time. 99
Drama as a Speaking Tool 103
Activities Addendum 107
Activities for Ages Two, Three, and Four 109
Activities for Ages Five, Six, and Seven 119
Survey Data 131

Introduction

Did you ever dream of speaking to a large group of people? Perhaps you wonder what it is like to receive a standing ovation because the message truly moved your listeners to action. Do you every think about the impact your feelings about speaking may have on your children? Is it possible that you want them to be the kind of leader you dreamed about and never became? Do you fear that the anxiety you feel is contagious and somehow affects your children? The facts are clear that a large percentage of adults just like you experience high levels of anxiety when they think about speaking to an audience.

You may have experienced shortness of breath, a burning sensation in your chest, or you broke into a sweat just picking up this book and realizing it is about public speaking. The fear is real…and misunderstood. You have always thought you have something important to share with the world and felt that you should overcome the fear and speak up. It is a feeling you have, a little voice that says, "I am important, and people need to know how I feel about my area of expertise." You wait for the moment and then avoid opportunity. You wander bookstores looking at all the how-to books on public speaking. You bought a special journal so you could record your ideas for transfer to the speech that makes a difference. You even bought the recorded speeches by John F. Kennedy and Dr. Martin Luther King thinking you would receive some inspiration.

Books tell you how to research, write, practice, and deliver a speech. However, you keep hearing some nagging voice in the back of your head that says, "I am not good at this. Now what do I do?" Perhaps you hear the voice of the one speech teacher you had in the one speech class you were required to take in high school. You hear her say, "You speak too fast," or "You have too many Ahs," or "You don't stand right," or "You speak too softly," or...and you believe the *can't do it* while ignoring the *can*.

You would love to receive large fees to speak at conferences and ultimately become a famous keynote speaker. Being famous is an admirable goal, but all you really want is to be able to translate the feelings in your heart and the knowledge in your head into a speech that moves people. It is common to tell yourself that your children will be better at the skill than you are or ever will be. Those five-to-seven-minute required speeches about vacations, favorite sports or hobbies, or demonstrating the art of pan-frying fish just do not satisfy the desire to talk about the way you feel about important issues in your life. The way you felt when your parents divorced, the anger experienced when a drunk driver injured your brother, or how a coach helped you realize your full potential.

As a parent, you recognize that your fears can easily transfer to your children, and you wonder how you can avoid that from happening. The child who was never afraid to cry out when hungry, injured, or wet may develop a quiet approach to communication, and you feel it might be your fault.

I wrote this book for you. Teaching has been my lifelong ambition. After many sidetracks from education, I am taking this opportunity to teach through the written word as well as through public speaking. My experiences in the college classroom and in businesses throughout the USA have given me insights into the anxiety associated with speaking in a public setting. I am also aware that you, parents and teachers, heavily influence children. My students have written specific examples of times that a parent or significant adult in their lives said or did something that caused them to stress over the very idea of speaking. In the classroom, I encourage those same students to recognize the affect they will someday have on their own children or students. I suggest that they become more positive while speaking or talking about speaking. It is a tough assignment, but like all attempts to make society more productive and positive, it takes effort.

I wrote the ideas and concepts in this book with the dream that something in it will move you to take action. The activities in the book addendum will require you to become an active participant in the development of speaking skills in children. Do not be afraid. Release your personal inhibitions and be a confident, courageous, and encouraging role model.

There is no doubt that leadership from you now and in your child's future will require more than just being an actor at the lectern. Affective leaders cannot be reticent or afraid to share very important messages with their audience. It is incumbent on parents and teachers to encourage the little people in their lives to move confidently from the Playground to the Podium.

Myths about Public Speaking

The college freshman stood, by all outward appearance, confidently at the front of my speech class. Fear was evident, but he was speaking. I thought he would actually speak the entire five-to-seven-minutes. Regrettably, he looked up from his manuscript and into the eyes of his fellow classmates. His face turned ashen, his eyes rolled up in their sockets, he passed out, fell forward, and gashed his head on the edge of a desk. This experience made me believe that a book about starting early to eliminate fear of speaking is essential. The student's story is told in full later in the book. Do not search now. You will get there.

Public Speaking Causes Fear...The Myth
It is odd that somewhere between the moments our children say their first word and pass puberty, they develop a fear of public speaking. It is true; we Americans fear public speaking more than any other phobia. People fear speaking to groups more than they fear snakes, spiders, heights, storms, or even dying. Anxiety associated with speaking may have a more permanent effect on human beings in our society than any fear. The positive influences from possessing the ability to speak in public likewise have a long-lasting effect.

Ask the people who are hiring staff to fill important positions in America's companies, and you will find that one of the major categories in the selection process is the person's ability to communicate. There is a concern that people must communicate not only with peers and management, but also with the public. Many truly successful people in corporate America have the competence to speak in public with minimal fear. Those who have succeeded without the ability often find it to their advantage to employ a spokesperson who can deliver the message with confidence to the public.

Behaviorist and educational researchers have conducted and published surveys over the past few decades repetitively estimating between ten and twenty percent of the American population experiences extreme levels of fear while speaking in public. The studies reveal that perhaps another twenty percent experiences apprehension at levels less extreme, but high enough to affect communication behavior negatively. Leaders in the field of communication apprehension research believe the consequences deserve attention. Apprehension about public speaking may be the most all-encompassing communication problem in our modern society.

Most Fears are learned

Because most fears are learned, it is a reasonable assumption that the vast majority of the population has learned that public speaking causes fear. Fortunately, you already have children who talk or soon will be talkers and walkers. You vividly remember the first word the child uttered. You may have documented the words in a baby book. It was probably "Dada," "Mama," "Bottle," or "No." Remember when the word first passed the lips of your child; you gave the equivalent of a standing ovation. You applauded, made cute faces, and sounded high-pitched accolades. You called Grandma and Grandpa, who promptly repeated the rave review. Your little person was instantly on stage, and everyone who entered your domain became the audience.

Guests and family who visited your home cued a curtain call for the little person to perform. Perform they did. Picture it this way, Mom and Dad standing proudly to the side spotlighting the star of the moment.

"Say 'Dada' for Mr. and Mrs. Browning, honey," they chide. "Come on now, say 'Dada.'"

Occasionally, the child will respond and make his or her parents very proud, but when the reaction is negative, the results can be detrimental. For example, one student in my speech class at Texas Christian University understands the way other people can influence one's view of public speaking. In this case, a speech teacher in high school emphasized what was wrong rather than what was right.

> A negative memory I have about public speaking is giving a presentation of a project that I had worked very hard on. The project looked great, but I got points taken off because of my presentation. The teacher laughed and pointed out to the class that I was obviously nervous. I was embarrassed and she counted off for it, which did not help my fear of public speaking.
>
> Katie

Programming Fear

When there is no response to "Say 'Dada' for Mr. and Mrs. Browning, honey," "Come on now, say 'Dada,'" the next comment is the first step toward programming a child to be afraid. "Oh, she is so shy," or worse, Mr. Rasco in my hometown used to say, "What's the matter, cat got your tongue?" What an ugly thought. It is little wonder that children develop a negative view of public speaking early in life. Simple changes in the way we parent and support a child can offset the learned fear process.

Many parents have their own ideas about the way they will raise their children long before birth. Among all the dreams for a great family is a personal dedication to the cause. You, too, may have decided to take parenthood seriously and made up your mind to do a good job. It is evident that the majority of parents start out with a view of parenting that is overly simplistic. Suddenly, reality hits like a rolling boulder and awakens you to the realization that raising children is difficult.

The size of the package has little to do with the accompanying emotions that you bring to the task of raising children. It is amazing that someone so small can cause such huge combinations of joy, excitement, love, and delight mixed with worry, guilt, frustration, and doubt. You get tired and overwhelmed by the task that stretches before you like endless barber pole spirals. Each problem is new, and the only thing consistent about the job is the change.

In spite of it all, you trust your instincts and move forward. All along the way, you invest heavily in time spent caring about the things you can give your child. You start college funds, buy the current clothing styles, prepare healthy meals, provide educational toys, and drive the neighborhood taxi service just as you are expected to do. When it all comes down to the bottom line, you question decisions because your child is just not developing the way you envisioned.

No one familiar with sports icons will deny the basketball capabilities of "Pistol" Pete Maravich. His many fans and I were saddened by his early death, but I have always remembered something he said in an interview February 25, 1977, after he scored sixty-eight points in a game against the New York Knicks. The journalist asked him about his ability to score so easily. I am paraphrasing his comment because I only wrote these words in a journal that day, "I don't remember ever missing." At the time, I thought that Maravich was sharing some secret to life with me. To start out in childhood being successful at something makes it easier as we grow older.

The Critical Nature of Family Influence

My brother, who played all star-quality basketball in college at Rice University, was a strong influence in my life. He built a basketball goal for me that was short enough that I did not get discouraged by shooting at a goal beyond my capability. When I consistently hit shots at the lower levels, he moved it up, never out of reach, but always enough to keep me challenged. He provided enough encouragement that I could consistently score at regulation height ten feet off the hardwood floor. "Pistol" Pete Maravich's father was his coach in college, and I suspect he somehow made sure that Pete would never remember missing. It crystallized my belief that big people in a child's life have a profound effect on success or failure.

"Pistol" Pete Maravich grew up not knowing that he would lead the nation in scoring but with an ingrained knowledge that he could never miss. It is clear that his self-esteem, belief in his capabilities, and unstoppable attitude made him one of the all time great basketball players. Not all children will grow to the stature of a Pete Maravich, but with parental encouragement and goal setting, the chances of success in public speaking grow incrementally.

Develop High Self-Esteem and Communication Confidence

A wonderful friend, and single parent, called me often during the first five or six years of her child's life to ask questions about her decisions regarding the way she disciplined, and schools she chose for her son. If quality is based on the effort that went into choosing the things that affected Steven's upbringing, he was destined for gold-plated excellence. He was given every opportunity to mature and develop into an exceptional individual.

Dianne was always capable of making decisions on her own, and, in most cases, she was on target with the choices she had already made. She simply sought someone to reaffirm her actions. As is true with most parents, the nagging questions about whether or not she was doing a good job rang loudly in her mind. The anticipation is much like the jack-in-the-box toy from my childhood days. Parents just keep turning the handle waiting for their child to pop out of their restrictive box and become a smiling, happy, and successful adult.

Even if your child is emotionally stable, runs with an equally balanced group of other youngsters, and demonstrates maturity, a quick glance at any daily newspaper makes a parent cringe at the possibilities. The headlines tell the parent that drugs, incurable diseases, and weapons in the classroom influence children despite the best parental decisions and intentions.

With those thoughts in mind, parents still want what is best for their children. They attempt to instill confidence, a sense of purpose, positive relationships, and the ability to succeed in classrooms and later in chosen professions. I believe that two critical requirements to succeed are the *Level of Self-Esteem* and the *Ability to Communicate Effectively*.

I have addressed public speaking anxiety in a way that will help promote confidence and basic speaking skills. As you progress through this book, you will understand the process that helps bring about self-esteem. Many of the specific components that lead a child to conclude she is both lovable and capable will be addressed. By using the exercises from this book and providing the positive feedback that is essential to good mental health, you will put in motion the confidence and techniques necessary for dynamic presentation skills.

Be prepared to lose your own inhibitions! Become a part of the exercises and let down the protective barriers that may keep you fearful of presenting ideas to others from the platform. Some of the skits and games ask you to do things that may seem childlike. However, by returning to those childlike behaviors, you stand a better chance to significantly influence the self-esteem of your child and increase your and your child's creative imagination.

One set of parents, Ryan and Millie, shared their own speaking skill changes after working with their child and attending a basic speech-training event at their company. Both had examples of times they ran off the stage or vomited when speaking to an audience. They transferred personal anxiety to their children and that was not acceptable to them. Millie said, "I have started breathing correctly when I speak, and I make sure I am prepared. Now I do not have the same anxious moments when I speak." Adults who practice these new skills regularly will have a positive influence on their children. It just takes effort.

Costs of Gaining a Competitive Edge

Over the years, I have taught public speaking classes to businesses, executives, and leaders. The training is expensive, but I am repeatedly told that the investment is worth it.

In an effort to gain a competitive edge in the world of business, adults who lack both self-esteem and speaking skills spend millions of dollars annually. Money and time are spent in an attempt to unlearn the negative feelings about oneself, reduce the anxiety associated with speaking in public, and relearn the skills that are generally inherent in children.

The more researchers study the phenomenon of success, the more they find that individuals with high levels of self-esteem, good interpersonal communication skills, and the ability to speak and write confidently may be the most likely to succeed in life. The question is why people wait until they are in a profession to fight their way out of their fears. Parents may think it is too late for them, but children are more likely to overcome the fears in the formidable years. And, for the record, I do not believe it is ever too late to personally improve speaking skills.

A chorus often sung among youth groups repeats the words, "I am Lovable and Capable." The words introduce us to two characteristics that every individual must feel in order to be a contributor in this society. It is evident that young people who sense an inner peace from being a lovable and capable personality are likely to select a positive set of friends, compete with confidence, and assume leadership roles in the group.

Being Lovable and Capable

Children and teens without the sense of being lovable and capable often make efforts to be like their peers who exude those traits. However, their attempt at a show of confidence tends to come across as loud, obnoxious conceit. Young people who possess the belief that they are lovable and capable assume a quiet air of confidence that does not require activity that is more boisterous. They simply radiate contentment with their beliefs, attitudes, and values and live them fully.

Young men and women, who were confident leaders in my church youth groups, have now assumed leadership roles in their communities, churches, education institutions, civic organizations, and political groups. Much of their success can be attributed to their willingness to speak both publicly and in small group settings. I always believed the students should be in leadership roles in the group, lead group sessions, and speak their opinions in every discussion. Participation was always encouraged and efforts, no matter how well articulated, received applause.

Help them be Lovable and Capable

A child's perception of personal satisfaction with their own self influences productivity, ability to get along with other people, and confidently choose friends and ultimately marriage companions. Being aware of this phenomenon, you may ask yourself, *How do I help my child become lovable and capable?* The importance of self-esteem and communication ability in your child's life cannot be overemphasized, and methods must be sought that instill a well-grounded belief in their personal skills.

Children Are Unique

"I am lovable" comes from the child's belief that he or she is unique and does not have to be like everyone else. It is the ability to feel loved by those who are most influential in the child's life parents, teachers, significant others, and peers.

Feeling loved is not the same as being loved. Children cry out for the feeling of love in the middle of extravagant gifts, nice clothing, and immaculate houses. All of these are symbols of being loved, but each lacks the touching and soft-spoken praises that clearly allow children to feel loved.

Once the sensation of being loved is evident, the child turns to the challenge of being capable. Learning that they are capable comes from the rewards given by parents and other family members early in life. The combination of loving, praising, and rewarding go a long way toward developing high levels of self-esteem.

I am also convinced that the way parents work with their children to enhance speaking and performance skills will positively influence the way they lead America in the future.

Imagination Puts Your Stars in a Row

It is important for parents to help direct their children toward a self-image that will stay with them into the future. Napoleon Bonaparte said, "Imagination rules the world." It is obvious from history that he knew what he was talking about when he made that statement. Except for a small imagination lapse at Waterloo, he was well on his way to ruling the world.

"Imagination is more important that knowledge," said Dr. Albert Einstein. Who could argue the credibility of the author of that quote? Early in my speaking career, I used the title *Put Your Stars in a Row* for all of my motivational inspirational presentations.

The idea came from the son of best friends. The little five-year-old is now an adult, but his message that cold January night warmed my heart and should be an impetus for imagination in all human beings. Steven Stewart was a student at the local Museum School, a pre-school program for children. He was given an assignment to make a picture of the sky.

The project resources consisted of a piece of black construction paper, a yellow construction paper circle that was to be the moon, and ten "lick-and-stick" stars. Steven was to place the moon and stars on the paper to look like the sky. He chose to turn the paper landscape to make his sky. He glued the moon in the upper left corner of the paper. Next, he placed his stars in a straight line starting from the left edge of the paper and moving to the right with a slight drop at the edge of the page.

Like every proud parent, Steven's mother pinned her son's art along the wall in the hallway. When my wife and I arrived for one of our frequent visits to the Stewart home, we were taken on the usual tour of new creations from the young artist. At the sky picture, Steven's mother asked if I had any idea why Steven would put his stars in a row. I said, "I don't know. Did you ask him?" She said, "No, but you are the behaviorist, you ask him."

When he returned from a visit to Grandpa's house, I asked Steven to show me his room. We entered the wonder of a little boy's private world. I was welcomed into the room by Garfield the Cat pictures and toys, storybooks, a rocking horse, match-car racetracks, and fairy-tale character curtains with a bedspread to match. He showed me all his newest toys and talked about games and cartoon videos.

Steven led me into the hall to see his Museum School art. He carefully explained the brown glob of watercolor paint with the long, pointed nose and four sticks for legs was an armadillo. The continuous lines drawn all over another page was a tree, obviously observed and painted from the inside out. When we came to the sky picture, he quickly pointed and said, "That's the sky."

I said, "Steven, is that the way the sky really looks?"

"Oh no," he exclaimed.

"Then why does your sky have all of the stars in a row?" came my curious inquiry. With all the wisdom and vision of a person who had not been affected by Madison Avenue's desire for everyone to be alike, he said, "Because that's the way I want it."

What a wonderful thought.

Don't Let Childhood Dreams Vanish

For the first time in my adult life, I realized that many of my childhood dreams had vanished for the sake of what other people wanted. As much as my family had encouraged me to be creative and dream, negative messages had slipped in to remove those desires. For many years, my self-expectations of teaching and helping others improve their skills had been put on a back burner to simmer with no apparent finish.

Steven helped renew my vision and gave me the drive to return to the classroom to teach college students to speak better and to develop a positive self-image. It occurred to me that our education system encourages students to worry about examination scores and IQ tests. Exceptional teachers or youth leaders direct them toward improving their imagination. I believe that active imaginations are the means for becoming the best and most creative worker, manager, president, or business owner.

Children can be taught that winners in life think about and actively develop a positive self-image. A child learns that he can visualize being the best before it ever happens. Children can learn that they can act like a success by dreaming with pictures and words in a fascinating storybook portion of their mind. They will learn that, ultimately, those pictures and words are drawn out in the form of new products and innovations. Their mental pictures can be used to communicate the importance of their dream.

Impact of Family

> I believe the only reason I have any anxiety about public speaking is because my mother is deathly afraid of it.
>
> Travis

Personal credentials for writing this book began with loving parents and supportive brothers. I consider myself to be among the fortunate minority of people in America who never learned to fear public speaking.

My parents were nearing that wonderful time in an adult's life when their children move on to a life of their own. Tommie and Bertie were thirty-eight and thirty-seven respectively when I was born. They had already raised a family of three. My brothers were ages thirteen, fifteen, and seventeen the year of my birth. But the beauty of my upbringing was that everyone listened to me; brothers, father, mother, the old dog, "Teddy," who I was named after, and even the milk cow were forced to listen to a little boy's constant banter while daily deeds and chores were in progress.

Early in life, I learned to tell stories and was encouraged to love speaking to any audience. The family's insistence on letting my imagination run free was a major contributor. Admittedly, the stories I told were often referred to as "whoppers," a good old West Texas term that meant "strong exaggeration."

Perhaps my imagination did run a little wild, but who says, "God and the devil never had a foot race, and God won." Mom would say, "Now that story is a bit unbelievable, but don't you love his imagination?" I remember the time she made me stop in the middle of a story I learned from a rodeo clown the night before. I know now it was not very nice, but a ten-year-old mind has little concept of naughty and nice. Perhaps Mom believed the audience was too sophisticated for such a fable.

Does Your Child Have a Positive Picture?

Children who are encouraged to talk about what they want to do in life are likely to realize that dream as an adult. Talking with a parent about becoming a musician, firefighter, or racecar driver helps create a picture in their mind. They soon know that who they feel like is who they really are as they become adults. It is sad that some parents, teachers, and student leaders hold back children who "are" by telling them what they "are not."

Human tendencies are to respond not to reality, but to their perception of reality. If the perception that a child will never be a success as a speaker is drummed into their mental computer, a small percentage of them may choose to overcome the picture, while others will simply never succeed. They stand a greater risk of perceiving themselves as a frightened person who may pass out when speaking in public.

How a child feels about himself is everything. For all he will ever do in life or think about in life will be based on the all-encompassing self-image. I am convinced that the human mind accepts what it has been conditioned to accept.

I have a friend who lost the end of his little finger in a lawnmower accident. For years after the accident occurred, he often experienced pain, itching, or other feelings where the finger should have been. He played the piano before the finger was severed. He told me that he continued to try to depress a key with a fingertip that no longer existed. Years of mental conditioning to use that finger at the keyboard caused the usual touch sensations, but without making a sound. He quickly learned to compensate and change his playing style. He had to adjust his picture of the skill to compensate for the missing finger.

The same principle applies to public speaking. A skill that is innate in most of us can be severed by a negative comment from a respected person. When that occurs, the child must find ways to compensate for the loss. Often, the way to deal with it is to withdraw from speaking opportunities, hide their face when the teacher is calling for a response, or experience the physiological symptoms associated with anxiety. Each time they cannot breathe during a presentation or shake uncontrollably before beginning to speak, the negative influences solidify the fear and cause more separation from opportunities. Parents and teachers have methods at their disposal to encourage behavioral modification. If the behavior is changed from negative to positive, the more likely the picture will change and the child will experience improvement. It takes support and practice to modify a negative belief to a positive action.

Overcome the Negative Pictures

The power of the human mind also internalizes perceptions that can seldom be eliminated without effort. Every humiliation or triumph, loss or win that children experience can have a lasting effect on the view the child has of self-image.

Self-image is susceptible to external forces. Young children who are treated as slow or inept may assume that they are inferior. Consequently, they internalize a negative picture and grow to be less than their potential. The images internalized over the years seem to be born out as proof of inadequacies.

At the little church in my small farming-community home, I sang with my friends from the time I could talk and walk to the front of the sanctuary. After church, the adults would tell us what a great job we did. I memorized the folk songs that were popular at the time and sang them as often as I could. Being a farm boy, I seldom had any human audience, but I pictured myself being a singer.

One day in my junior high school choir room, my picture faded. I decided to try out for the male chorus. When I stood before the choir director, he played a scale and asked me to sing it. A student with the best voice in the whole school was there assisting the director. Not only was he the best in school, he had earned state competition honors. He was an exceptional talent, and I was in awe of his skills.

The director played the scale, and I proudly opened my mouth and sang, "La, La, La, La, La, La, La, La." Maybe I should have watched *The Sound of Music* a few more times and really learned "Do Re Me Fa So La Ti Do" to improve my singing skills. Unfortunately, I had not. I sang as boldly as I knew how. When the best voice in school heard me sing the scale, he snickered and ultimately laughed out loud when I sang "La, La" way off key on the high notes. I was embarrassed that day. I find it frightening now that I can remember the positive strokes I received from my church family, but I stopped singing because of one snicker from a peer I respected.

> I was reading in front of the church. The paper said, "Pause for about 30 seconds." I read it aloud to the congregation and it was supposed to be a side note to me. The congregation laughed, and I saw the embarrassment in my father's eyes. I'll never forget it.
>
> Meredith

Meredith's and my experiences are common. Regrettably, the same scenario is played out in schools, churches, homes, and on playgrounds throughout our country daily. Our children and we internalize the negative input from others and perceive that we must not be quality. It was all based on the comments, non-verbal cues, and noises from other people.

You have heard people say things like "I remember faces, but I can never remember names." When they meet someone who looks familiar, they immediately try to remember the name. When they open their mental directory searching for the name, the brain has the information but will not let them have it. I am convinced that all the names of people introduced to me are in my brain as surely as are their images. The repetitive reinforcement from saying, "I cannot remember names," defeats the fact that the name is there to be retrieved.

The more a person says, "I am a terrible speaker," the more their mind believes the statement…a terrible speaker they will be. Each of us is controlled by the mental pictures we form, and are formed for us by other people in our lives. It is important that parents emphasize the positive in their children rather than dwell on the negatives.

The innate power a child possesses from infancy forward is often influenced by the negative feedback from people we love and respect. Knowing the potential effect on a child should make us all more aware of the power of positive feedback. Parents, teachers, youth leaders, and others of significance can truly make a difference in the lives of our future leaders. They help improve a child by instilling ritual and routine into their lives. A disciplined life with specific goals has a greater chance of being a positive influence to others.

The Positive Approach to Discipline

When most people hear the word *discipline,* they immediately think of negative, overbearing comparisons such as spank, restrict, punish, force, or ground. What words come to your mind? Are they similar to the list mentioned here? Do you find yourself struggling with the concept of discipline based on the being harsh? If yes, the intent of this chapter is to change your view of discipline to a more positive, upbeat picture.

Interestingly enough, education is listed as a synonym when the word *discipline* is found in dictionaries. However, education or teaching is not typically considered when the word *discipline* is mentioned in conversation strategies.

Training that Strengthens

My personal desire is to teach all parents to replace their concept of discipline to a more positive dictionary definition: *training that strengthens.* So many parents try to reach that goal by methods that fit another meaning: punishment or control by force.

I like to think of the word *disciple* when discussing the method parents should use for disciplining. According to the *Oxford Pocket Dictionary and Thesaurus,* one of the definitions of *disciple* is "a follower of a teacher." We do not think of a disciple following his teacher out of fear of punishment, but rather from inner conviction. Parents and teachers should learn to expect children to follow rules because they believe in them, rather than because they fear retaliation. Anytime a child has a ritual or routine that leads toward following rules, it is easier for him to have self-control for mental or physical training. The key goal is self-discipline.

To prepare for the world, our children will face overwhelming choices. Whether they choose a profession that keeps them in a keyboard environment or speaking to a board of directors, they must learn to self-discipline. The activities and parenting strategies written in this book encourage active participation on the part of parent and child. The intent is to create disciplined habits that will be beneficial throughout life.

Rules work toward self-regulation and enhanced self-image when emotionally embraced. Herein lies the secret to constructive discipline. When parents and teachers help children understand that order in their lives produces positive learning opportunities, children grow more confident.

To enhance self-esteem and encourage speaking in public, the limitations set by restrictive rules that limit creativity must be removed. Parents must answer some basic questions, such as: How are rules enforced constructively? Who establishes the rules? The answer is found in the word *disciple*. Children are the learners and parents and teachers are the inspiration for learning.

Discipline by punishment tends to hold aversive consequences: physical pain, grounding, isolation, loss of privileges. A problem with punishment alone is that it does not teach the child what he or she is to do, and only what he or she is not to do. I believe that heavy reliance on punishment leads to feelings of guilt, resentment, and hostility. A physical punishment, such as hitting, teaches lessons that should not be a part of the child's learning experience. When hitting occurs, a child learns that you have to be bigger, and stronger to have the upper hand in the situation.

Power of Rewarding: What this Chapter is Truly About
Rewards, on the other hand, direct the child to the behavior that is desired and make it likely that good behavior will happen again. Rewards can include praise, time with parents, a fun family activity, a toy, a sticker, or some other item or privilege. My daughter-in-law and son keep small toys or treats just out of reach but visible for my granddaughter to choose from when good behavior or new skills are demonstrated.

Reward is different from a bribe. A bribe is something given or promised ahead of time for not doing something. A reward is given afterwards for doing something right. Ask yourself the question, "Do I more often bribe or reward?"

In parenting and teaching, it is impossible to avoid punishment totally. However, parents can remember that positive rewards lead to positive behavior, and positive behavior leads to stronger self-image.

Adults feel positive when we have used good self-control and have gotten up early for exercise, read two self-help chapters daily, or when we have finished a project that we determined to complete in minimal time. Like these adult examples, children learn that a self-disciplined life can be rewarding. They become disciplined learners within themselves not because punishment is imposed on them. We all want children to behave as well when we are not with them as when we are. Positive behaviors are expected when your children are away from your influence and when you are in the room with them.

Give Reasons for Good Behavior

Telling children sensible reasons for behaving in certain ways helps them understand that behaving in an appropriate manner is more than not being caught doing inappropriate things. We can teach our children by driving the posted speed even when no police are around because driving at or under the speed limit is safer than speeding. Talk to them about that ritual, and they will notice the positives.

Children who receive positive feedback from parents and teachers for speaking in public are more likely to be effective communicators. Those who are criticized for their "ums" and "ahs," stutters, mispronounced words, gestures, or body language have a reduced chance of being good in speaking situations.

In every college or professional class I teach, I emphasize what the speaker is doing well. When the student sees a video of their speech, I point out possible improvements but take time and extra effort to show what he or she did well. The *done well* often overcomes, and marked improvement is evident by the end of the class.

Expectations and Trust

Teachers, youth leaders, or parents do not try to create problems in children. When unexpected safety issues occur, we are genuinely bewildered, but we just cannot cover all the variables when establishing expectations. With our sons, it was the time they rode their bicycles seven miles down a busy highway. The two were accompanied by neighborhood friends to buy fireworks for the Fourth of July. I had said that fireworks could be purchased and felt the implication that I should be with them was evident. It was not. We did not specifically say, "Don't ride your bicycles on the highway." Their mother and I believed they would never even think about the possibility. You know issues you face with failing to communicate expectation clearly and can easily add your own stories here.

Most of us are unaware that internal strife builds when children do not feel safe or clearly know the rules. To consider that we have failed to provide safety is a total shock to most of us. Regrettably, we usually think of safety only in physical terms and have few ideas what makes up a safe environment in the minds of our children. In my opinion, children who have a clear understanding of what is expected will have a more trusting relation with parents and teachers.

Cast Off Imaginary Masks
Without the positive feelings about themselves, children learn to wear imaginary masks and begin to feel alienated. They may even develop defenses that protect them from the lack of a safe

mental feeling. Children may create imaginary playmates, find special hiding places, or dream up some of the most phenomenal make-believe stories during their daily routine. I am convinced that a developing imagination is a critical part of a child's growth. It will influence their future as successful communicators and leaders. I was never able to differentiate between my children's imaginations that were used as masks and imaginations that were creative and fun. To me, it did not matter. I felt that imagination that was accepted and an integral part of the child I loved was okay.

> When I was a little boy, I made believe that I was entertaining a lot of people. I would stand in front of my dresser mirror in my room and pretend to be a singer. I pretended I had backup singers and a band. One day my mother came into my room and surprised me. I had been singing and talking to my imaginary band and didn't even know she was in the room. I was upset at first, but I always did it just to get away. I believe it helped me be more confident as a speaker now that I'm older.
>
> Greg

Our children have grown into stable and successful adults. My wife and I are proud of that fact and are pleased that confident grandchildren have been added to the family. No parent can provide a consistently safe climate for all children all the time. Supporting a child and believing in his or her ability can be overwhelming. I know I am not perfect, but through the blessings of God and a supportive family, the parenting job has been relatively easy. It is important to know that children are pliable and generally survive in spite of our shortcomings.

Children Are Adaptable and Tough

All of us have various traits that, hard as they are to face, sometimes harm those we love. Living in the close quarters of the family inevitably causes hurts. This is an unpleasant fact. Fortunately, most children are not overly fragile and survive the pendulum swings of family living. Their physical and mental pains heal and they prove their resilience daily. They are pushed from inside themselves to develop self-respect, and when they are given half a chance, they will.

Every child is born into a position of not knowing anything about expectations. Children do not initially think in these terms, but early experiences let the child know whether he can count on parents and teachers for assistance in meeting his physical and emotional needs. Parents set the expectations, and they trust us to help them grow physically and, more importantly, emotionally stable.

Children Need to Trust

Without trust in parents, siblings, the family pet, friends, and extended family, growth rests on emotional quicksand that affects all future development. I believe infants experience their needs as intense and immediate. They have little tolerance if fast action is not taken. Our grandchildren are on schedules that meet each child's needs. We grandparents should learn to respect the desires of our sons and daughters-in-law to maintain schedules that help the babies feel safe.

We never set a specific time for our sons to go to bed, but because they trusted us to care for their physical and mental needs, we seldom had to worry about it. Parenting books on the bookshelves today emphasize specific scheduling. We did not set schedules and survived, but I am a believer in the principles outlined in today's parenting guides.

Children Sense Parents' Tensions

Some parents are walking bundles of tension, and their babies sense it. Children quickly pick up friction between parents, spoken or otherwise. When that occurs, tension springs out of the emotional unrest. These must be worked through if youngsters are to feel safe.

Early in life, a child may sense Dad or Mom's tension before speaking. There is no hard evidence, but my students have often reported knowing and feeling that their parents were extremely afraid to speak in public. Some report that their own anxiety may come from parental influence.

Trust is built in many ways. We felt it was important to let our sons know when and where we were going and when we would return. It was important to avoid sudden, unpleasant surprises. If we were visiting a dentist, doctor, or some other perceived scary place, we discussed what they could expect.

Sometimes the surprises slip up on us. On a visit to Disney World, Kevin, age four at the time, noticed one of the seven dwarfs sitting on a fountain ledge. Kevin's natural inquisitiveness led him to walk up the steps to see why the character was sitting so still. Sleepy woke with a start when Kevin touched his leg. The sudden movement frightened Kevin, and he rolled down the three short steps attempting to get away. It was years before Kevin would have anything to do with any creature that resembled a sleeping dwarf. Suppose the tension he felt over a sleeping dwarf had been caused by a frightening, speaking situation he observed. Here is what one of my students wrote.

When the dog bit my brother, I was frightened and still fear dogs. My mother was speaking at a school PTA event and I saw her start crying and run off the stage. I was not directly influenced by either event, but I believe to this day that I fear both because of what I saw, not what I experienced.

No name

I agree with the student's observation. Parents are faced with unbelievable pressure to influence children positively. Public speaking is threatening to many people, so positive influence is more difficult when the action is painful emotionally.

Children Sense Parents' Feelings

I believe it is vital to avoid promises impossible to keep. When golf gets in the way of a promised trip to the zoo, the resulting negative feelings can last a long time. Children have high expectations for honesty and integrity from people they respect. A broken promise once can lead to distrust in the future.

Most of us would never knowingly build distrust, but may unknowingly do so by failing to be honest with our child about our feelings. It can happen in many subtle ways. The method does not matter; it is the mixed message the child receives that makes all the difference.

Children sense the anxiety. A friend told me about working in his garage one Saturday morning. He had experienced a bad week at work, and his wife had asked him to finish the clean-out-the-garage job he started the month before. He said he had been throwing things around, sweeping the garage with a vengeance, and had the kind of look on his face that said, "I'm hacked off, don't say a word to me." When his daughter came out to be with her daddy, she immediately sensed something was wrong. She asked, "What's the matter, Daddy?"

"Nothing," he snapped. "I'm just fine." Well, the words may have said that all is well, but the body language and vocal forcefulness presented a whole other picture.

He told me that his daughter knew him well enough not to say anything more. I asked what he thought she was saying to herself as she went on about her Saturday morning. Could it have been, "Gee, I wonder if he found that paint I spilled on the floor behind the lawnmower? Or is he mad about something else I've done?"

His daughter's confusion is understandable. She has received two messages: one from her daddy's words, "Nothing's wrong," and a contradictory one from his body and tone of voice, "Something is very definitely wrong." Whenever words do not match up to body language, a child feels trapped by the mixed messages. The confusion pushes her into second-guessing what may really be happening.

Every child first learns to rely on nonverbal clues. When they conflict with verbal messages, the son or daughter naturally gives the nonverbal priority. The child counts on them but still has to deal with the words.

The problem is that how a parent really feels is evident in nonverbal communication. You probably know this from your own experience. If your wife says, *Of course you should watch the game with your friends,* you pick up on her plans to get her way almost immediately. If your husband plays Mr. Handy, you find out soon enough that it may just be a plan to actually go to the game with the guys. We cannot live with others, particularly children, day after day and fool them about our true feelings. Abraham Lincoln was right about fooling the people. As the president noted, "You can't fool all the people all the time." This is certainly evident in a close-knit family environment.

Hiding Inner Feelings

I have known couples that play the role of "anything-you-want-dear" parents even when deep inside they are quite opposed to some of the things their children do. They hide their inner feelings with phony words, but their resentments build up inside until they break out in the form of sarcasm, or what I like to call "plastic smiley faces."

An added disadvantage to mixed messages is that children merge their personal concerns into the puzzle. In our earlier example, the little girl, already feeling guilty about the spilled paint, probably believed that her secret caused her daddy's anger. However, if her primary concern had been doubt over his love, she could have read this anxiety into the dual messages. She could have thought, *I guess Daddy is not happy to see me this morning. Maybe he wishes he didn't have me for a daughter.* The possibilities are endless, but the knowledge that the message is received incorrectly can be invaluable when the parent reconsiders the words and actions. Accepting responsibility for one's actions and words can go a long way in solving rifts between parent-child relationships.

This same principle applies when a parent inadvertently snickers or grimaces when his or her child makes an error in public speaking. I am convinced that children who see the nonverbal negative feedback are more influenced by that moment than by hundreds of positive comments.

Honesty Nurtures Relationships

The single most important ingredient in a nurturing relationship is honesty. Probably one reason most of us enjoy young children so much is that they are real. When they are mad, we know it. When they are happy, they send the message loud and clear. Parents just know where we stand with them by the message they send verbally and through body language.

We do not have uneasy feelings with real friends. We tend to treasure those we can trust because we feel safe. I believe children respond the same way. We must learn to be as honest with them as they are with us.

I attended a family reunion several years ago. We finished a big country lunch consisting of fried chicken, potatoes and gravy, and a hundred other items that tended to be stuck in the mustache I wore back then. About an hour after I finished eating, I picked up my five-year-old niece, Mary Vonda. As I carried her around, she kept looking at my face. I finally asked her what she was looking at. She said, "Uncle Teddy, you got gunky on your mustache." The sad thing about the scene is not Mary Vonda's honesty, but the failure of my closest adult family members who let me go through life with gunky on my mustache. Yes, there is innate honesty in children and, regrettably, we adults have decided we would rather be courteous than honest even for friends and family with gunky on them. This is not a license to be rude, but it is a plea to be honest in a positive way.

Avoid Sending Mixed Messages

Sending mixed messages is a habit that must be broken. Many of us fall into it through imitating others. We may choose this path fearing disapproval if we express honest feelings. We may hesitate to expose ourselves or fear dealing with certain emotions. Sometimes we give phony responses because it is easier than trying to get in touch with our real feelings. At other times, we cover up because we are afraid that our openness may hurt others. Too much is at stake, however, for you not to make an all-out effort to avoid telling your family and your children about the gunky in their mustaches.

How can you avoid mixed messages when you really do not want to share your feelings? Let us go back to my angry friend and his daughter. Perhaps he simply did not want his little girl to know that he was upset over the argument with her mother or with what was happening at the office. He could have said, "Honey, I'm upset about a grown-up problem that I don't want to talk about just now." Those words coupled with something like, "But I love you. Do you want to help me sweep the garage?" would have helped match his words and body language. When these match, the child is not confused by contradictions. If she were anything like my sons, she would have said, "No, I'll just go get some juice and watch cartoons." That would be okay.

What if he had found the spilled paint but felt that he bad been upset with his daughter too much lately. One part of him may want to vent frustration, while another part feels it would be easier to say nothing.

It Is How You Say It that Counts

He could say, "I'd rather not discuss what's bugging me." Then he risks internalizing little things that may cause him to blow up over something of little significance later on. The alternative is honesty about both sets of feelings. He could say, "I found the spilled paint, and it upsets me that you didn't tell me or your mother about the spill." Inside his head, he may be saying, *But it seems as if I've been upset with you so much that part of me hates to mention it. I am sitting on top of two feelings. One makes me so frustrated I want to scream, and the other makes me wonder if I expect too much.* Parents have the power to choose a path that comforts while reinforcing positive behavior.

Honesty Means Sharing Conflicting Feelings

Sharing conflicting feelings is part of honesty. Seldom do we have just one reaction to a situation. Two or more opposing feelings are more frequent. Because children are remarkably sensitive to emotional changes, sharing only part of our feelings confuses them.

You may choose to keep certain feelings to yourself, but be honest about your reservations. It is not appropriate to be totally open about all of your feelings with everyone at all times. You have to decide for yourself when, where, to whom, and how much of your inner world is appropriate to share. Regardless of your decision, be honest about your reservations and do not hide them. It is not healthy for you or your children.

Many of us believe that strong feelings are a sign of immaturity. Therefore, if we feel intensely, we soft-pedal the emotion to fit our image of the mature adult. In my hometown, boys were taught to hide disappointment, tenderness, or sorrow. I remember falling off my horse and trying with all my might to avoid crying because at eleven years old, I had learned that big boys do not cry. In addition to the hurt and the fact that I could not breath, I was lying at the feet of my older brother and my new sister-in-law. I wanted to be macho, and I did not even know what it meant. I was still a child, and eventually the tears flowed. Now I realize that it did not matter to my family. Their only concern was my health. I think that moment was a boost to my self-esteem because there was no rejection as I had anticipated.

The person with high self-esteem does not have to deny feelings. Self-acceptance gives the security to be open. It means not having to seek approval from others. Ownership of feelings is a critical element of high self-esteem.

I believe that children pick up the discrepancy when we use mild messages for strong feelings, but they do not know why we water them down. Many a child concludes, "It's not right to feel intensely. If I don't feel casual, I'd better pretend that I do."

I personally felt that way for a short time and until the pain and shortness of breath actually took over. I got back on my horse and trotted away because I received honest attention when I needed it most.

True Honesty Is Appropriate Honesty

Honesty does not mean making children emotional whipping posts. It is possible to match words to feelings and still convey an appropriate message. Once in a grocery store, I overheard a mother who had experienced a rough day, and her son's lack of cooperation was getting to her. I heard her say, "Oh, I wish I'd never had children!" The toddler was not able to understand the words. However, if they are repeated as he grows older, the message will sink in. I hoped that in the next setting she might have said, "I've absolutely had it today! I need to be alone for a while!" This response is honest; it expresses her need for time away from her son without damaging his self-respect.

This expression of honesty says, "You can count on me to help you meet your needs. I am not perfect, but you can depend on my being honest with you. It is okay for you to have flaws, too, and together we can grow stronger and more emotionally balanced." When the time comes for support in a child's drama or speaking situation, this kind of honesty will help reduce the anxiety associated with the consequence of the action.

Every child needs to know that they can believe what parents say and depend on them for friendly help in meeting any need. Being open with children is not enough, however. Whether you damage or build self-esteem depends upon how you tell children about your feelings. If they are to feel safe with you, you must communicate to them in non-judgmental ways.

Remember that it is okay to fear speaking to groups of people, but do not hide it. Children know when you are upset. It is best to say the way you feel, but reassure that the feeling does not have to be your child's inheritance. Encourage them to act, speak, sing, and play instruments as often as they will. I believe it is better for them to learn from experience than to learn from a parent's anxiety and following reaction. One of my students graphically emphasized the reverse of this belief.

> My fear in public speaking was caused by my mother and a few of church colleagues that always told me to walk properly. The people always told me to change the way I walked or told me I was stiff. That made me very conscious of myself in public and made me withdraw from public settings. As a result, I developed fear to speak in public settings.
>
> No Name

Use Positive Reinforcement

I remember taking my son Kevin to the dentist. I sat quietly while he and an assistant worked on my son's teeth. When finished, the dentist looked at me and said, "Your son was a good patient!" It sounded good to a father's ear, but how much better for Kevin's self-worth if the dentist had said, "Kevin didn't fuss about my working on him, which made it easier for me. Thanks, Kevin, for helping me out."

Countless books and articles urge parents and teachers to lean heavily on praise. I have personally always believed that praise was the most important part of raising my children and that it far outweighed punishment as an effective behavior changer. Children want positive affirmations from parents and teachers, and they will do everything they can to get them. I do and you do, so why shouldn't they?

The point is that to be confident, a child must not have to question his worth as a person. That must always be clearly understood. It is clear to a child when he is told that he is a good boy because you like what he did.

Children may learn to think of his behavior as synonymous with his person. Because behavior comes from the child just as heat rays come from the sun, it is easy to think, *Bad behavior, bad person; good behavior, good person.* Such thinking fails to separate a child from his acts. To criticize the person rather than the behavior is wrong.

Set Realistic Expectations

Whenever personal worth is dependent upon performance, personal value is subject to cancellation with every misstep. When I was expected to perform to the same level of performance in basketball that my brother did, I was destined to fail. I was a much better athlete with a horse under me than with a ball in my hands. A child's self-respect is unstable unless he manages to walk the tightrope of continuously high performance that some people come to expect of him.

No child always behaves in acceptable ways. When your attitudes and words equate his acts with his person, he lives a yo-yo-like existence. Up and down his personal value goes in accordance with his behavior. Even if you do not believe your child is what he does, your words can make him think so.

When your child lives with a caring and honest parent like you, he can say, "I am lovable even though not all of my behavior is acceptable." The healthy child sees his person as separate from his acts. A sense of personal value independent of behavior is essential to high self-esteem. How you talk to children affects whether they make the vital distinction between behavior and self.

Family Games Enhance Self-Esteem

Play games with your children. On many occasions after dinner, we took a spontaneous trip for snow cones or other treats and returned for some family games. My sons used to win against my wife and me in Chess games or Backgammon. My luck held on Hearts, Monopoly, and during their younger years, I could even win in Candy Land or Yahtzee.

It was obvious to me that games like Candy Land can teach kids valuable skills. Playing games can be a great way to teach social skills and improve your child's self-esteem. He probably will not know he is learning while playing games, but moving pieces around game boards offer lessons in basic math, social interaction, and more. When you play games together, you spend quality time and teach useful skills.

The combination of skill and luck make game-playing a great family activity. My wife and I started playing games with our two sons early. We changed some of the rules when they were small to make the game fun for everyone. We felt that the interaction around a game board brought family members close. When my parents were in town, we played dominoes because they enjoyed playing. Each boy got to play the domino he chose with a little coaching from a grandparent.

Some of my best childhood memories are of playing games in my little community. Often there were winter conditions that confined us to the house for extended periods. My mother would invite children and their parents to our home. We grew into Monopoly and Clue after a while, but I can remember hours of Sorry and Old Maid that were less taxing on preschool and early elementary minds.

Often we invented games and played them together. My mother was ahead of her time. She would cut out pictures of animals and ask us to act out the animal so we could guess what it was. It was charades without having to read the words, and it gave us an opportunity to be speaking and acting in public.

Now there is a game called *Kids on Stage* that does the same thing. (I found it on www.areyougame.com, but try your own sources) It is a great way for families to become an audience for children. Reading is not required for this charades game. The participants have cards with pictures that they can act out much as my mother did for me many years ago. The suggested age is three to seven, but from my experience, even the over-age-fifty group can quickly get into the action.

It affords the opportunity for children to hear accolades and applause without causing any negative feelings. These produce positive strokes that will remain with your child, perhaps for his lifetime. My student Kelly and her brother are evidence of this belief.

> My parents always encouraged my brother and me to entertain their friends. We would dress up and do skits that we just dreamed up on the spot. After a while, our parents helped us write our own short plays and we presented them when visitors were over. Our mom and dad always clapped and cheered us on. I remember feeling so good when we made them happy.
>
> Kelly

Make Time for Play

Finding time to play is sometimes difficult. One idea is to schedule a family game night as often as is comfortable for your family. When you attempt to play one night per week, it may be too much. Try to have a special night at least two times per month. Make it fun, have some snacks available, and the children and you will look forward to it.

In addition to strengthening family bonds, playing games together fosters learning. There are so many wonderful computer games designed to help your child with reading and math skills. Play along, encourage winning, and give positive accolades.

I believe that preschoolers can learn plenty from almost any game they play. Games teach basic social manners. Kids learn to wait for turns, share, and work together. There will be times when the game board will be upset because a child is impatient and wants every turn to be his. Patience and assurance that everyone will have his or her chance to play will pay off.

It is interesting to watch faces as children begin to develop compassion and empathy when family members or friends face challenges. Our son Kevin always wanted to help others when they were struggling with a board game move. He counted spaces, suggested that if they moved another way, they would not knock Daddy's piece off the space. It appears it also teaches respect for their elders.

Real Play is Invaluable

Outside activities are real indicators of your interest in the child. I believe the move to computer and interactive television has eliminated a very important part of a child's life. The mental exercise is great, but physical play seems to be happening less and less in families.

Parents who plan daily outdoor activities give their children an added benefit. Kicking a soccer ball, playing catch, riding bicycles, or just walking around parks and duck ponds aid in improving the physical health of parent and child.

Communication increases when in play. "Go out for a long pass!" "Great catch!" "You are awesome for playing with me!" "Thank you for making this afternoon so special!" The possibilities go on.

You can further enhance the child's skills when you ask him or her to tell others what the two of you (or the family) did when playing. Let them be graphic. The reward is great and speaking skills are nurtured.

Games Improve Thinking Skills

Game playing encourages critical-thinking skills. I often recommend that people who attend my public speaking classes begin to attend Toastmasters International meetings. Toastmaster is not for your pre-school-age child, but it can help you. The positive reinforcement you receive there may help your son or daughter see the "I am not worried" side of you.

I got in trouble with the dean of my department in one of the local colleges. A student explained to me that she was interested in politics and wanted to learn how to think quickly when asked about a political issue. She asked what class she should attend to improve this skill. I told her to save her money and go to Toastmasters. When that message got back to the dean, I was called into his office and informed that students attending classes helped pay me when I teach there. I received the message loud and clear, but secretly encouraged attending meetings.

I believe that game playing early on is a great way to encourage critical-thinking skills. Toastmasters have a segment called

Table Topics that allows a participant to speak for two minutes on a subject that they were given only seconds before. I am not sure that Toastmaster International leaders would consider it a game, but it is one event where people can compete against their own fears. By standing up to those fears in this demanding game, there is a chance to win.

I have seen people stand for two minutes with an embarrassed look and fright seeping out. I often wonder if they never had the opportunity to play games that enhanced thinking skills. Any encouragement parents can give increases the potential of avoiding the fears. Table topics are a great way to get children to talk as well.

Practice Voids Fear

The good thing is that practice overcomes the fear. I refer to it as the Eleanor Magalassi syndrome. Eleanor was in a Toastmasters Club, and on her first Table Topic, she did not say a word for two minutes, then she sat down and I led the applause. The next week she was there again and when her turn came, she stood up again and said nothing and sat down, and I led the applause.

I know this sounds like it could be painful, but the beauty of the Eleanor Magalassi syndrome is that it can be overcome. Every time she stood up and did not speak, she received the same applause and support as the Toastmasters who talked effortlessly for two minutes.

I believe we must focus on the strong points and avoid talking about what did not work. When strengths are emphasized, the person builds on what is right for them until they overcome the negative. Eleanor kept at it until she began to speak each time and ultimately won contests in Toastmasters competition.

I knew Eleanor in the 1980s and do not know what became of her, but I know she was a confident speaker when I last saw her perform. She once told me how much she appreciated the applause. I believe it was what made her keep working toward great speaking skills. The point here is that adults can experience thinking games as well. If you want to help your child, help yourself.

The Influence of Language Styles

It is important for parents to understand the significance of language on the young child. As the child grows and develops, the language skills they learn will benefit them.

I do not know that it is possible to state a precise age at which language in a child begins. It is obvious that during the first six months of life, most infants make a variety of noises when excited by parental entertainment, hunger, or those diapered inconveniences that infants have no control over nor the ability resolve.

In the course of babbling, crying, and cooing that occurs from the second month of life, the infant emits a number of sounds that form a part of their language. Meaningful words generally appear around one year of age, and the child can probably understand more items than he or she is capable of producing.

Words to Meaning
Human language enables us to communicate with others, and it provides the listener with an efficient means of internalizing their own interpretation of what has been stated. We often use language to communicate with ourselves. Think of the times you have mentally said, *Don't get in that water until checking it with my toe.* No verbal is necessary, even though we sometimes say it aloud, but the communication exists. What student in some bumbling old professor's college class has not internally said, *Gosh, this guy is boring. I wish I could just walk out of here.*

Those messages are a part of our being much the same as the hair on our head. The language we teach our children to use influences their development enormously. Language increases the scope of what can be accomplished and communicated internally. The symbolic system constitutes a kind of internal work making it possible for human beings to reason, to reflect, and to develop kinds of awareness that are inconceivable in other species. It is the parent's role to develop and nurture their children's learning-language skills.

I do not intend to answer the questions regarding the impact of language on learning or vice versa. Rather, the intent is to help realize that some relationship does exist, accept it as fact, and move on the primary objective to give our children positive reinforcement for communicating.

Children Interpret Early

When our sons were very small, Brent often interpreted what his younger brother had said. It amazed me that he could understand the unintelligible sounds and tell us what his brother needed. That experience taught me that the actual words are not necessary to communicate meaning.

During my stint in the U.S. Navy, my family shared our home with four sailors from Greece for one evening. Three of the four spoke no English at all, and the fourth had a very limited vocabulary. At the risk of sounding trite, their communication attempts were all Greek to me.

At dinner that evening, we managed to get everyone seated and started the meal. Soon after we began eating, one of the sailors said something. My wife and I immediately looked to the translator, who was lost for the words and resorted to pointing at something on my end of the table.

Without looking up, Brent said, "He wants the butter dish and knife." I picked up the dish, passed it down the table, and received a very happy "Thank you!" with an accent. Those two words may have been the only English the sailor spoke, but he had communicated with untrained ears on a very small child with ease. Brent had not yet learned that you could not reason through the sounds and gestures a person makes to understand needs. The older we get, the more we demand that others conform to what is clear to our minds. I find it interesting that we often raise our voices a few decibels while speaking in English to a person who does not understand a word. It appears that we believe a little volume and a few gestures will make them understand. The flaws in that belief are evident.

Help Develop Understanding

Developing understanding of the words often comes from the rewards associated with the word or phrase. Obviously, the word *bottle* is quickly associated with the reward of food. In addition to rewards, startling realizations of pain or other negative reinforcement helps assign meaning. It only takes one touch of something hot to assign the meaning of, "Don't ever do that again, it's hot!"

Messages sent to children without reinforcement, rewards, or the threat of injury take longer to internalize. If a father were to kneel before his child, who is just learning to crawl, and say, "Come to Daddy," the child will not associate the meaning of the words with what she is supposed to do. If no reward is offered, the father might as well suggest that Mount Rushmore should move to Texas. On the other hand, when a bottle, stuffed animal, or some other object of their affection is held up at the same time the words "Come to Daddy" are said, the results will be significantly different.

Teach Communication without Fear

The same principle applies to teaching a child to communicate without fear. Positive strokes for positive performance help the child accomplish the parent's objective. The more rapidly the child comprehends the languages that say, "You are very good at what you do," or, "You can do anything you want to do," will be a tremendous asset. The more frequently positive reinforcement is given, the more likely the feeling of self-worth will flourish.

It is unfortunate that some of the language a child internalizes early in life is negative in nature. Hearing a parent say, "Don't speak unless spoken to," or, "You're too young to have anything important to say," or, "Don't say that, that's dumb," can cause irreparable damage as the child goes off to school to make that first presentation in the classroom. Ashley had this to say about her experience,

> When I was a child, I vividly recall being silenced at dinner as the adults spoke to one another. Because my life experiences seemed trite in comparison to their business matters, I chose to not speak. Later, in social situations, I felt that if I didn't have something imperative to say, it was best to remain silent.
>
> Ashley

Behaviorists refer to the phenomenon we are discussing as operant conditioning or instrumental conditioning. The terms seem interchangeable in the literature, but the key is that regardless of the language used to identify the concept, the central driving force is reinforcement. A reinforcing event is one that raises the probability of a response that it regularly follows. I have mentioned the value of reinforcement and applause throughout this book. I will continue to write it. I believe a parent or teacher's positive reaction sets the stage for fearless behavior. Here is what Christina, a student from my speech class, had to say about the opposite feedback.

> I spoke to anyone and everyone and sometimes to my self. It wasn't until I was diagnosed with dyslexia by a teacher that this "stigma" was put upon me by peers and teachers. I was constantly made aware of my problem and that I spoke too frequently and without pauses. Slowly over time, I went from being bubbly and extroverted to a shy girl staring off into the corner hoping the teacher would not call on me to read. *See* the problem was never the disorder; it was the "stigma" that people think you cannot perform well.
>
> Christina

It is obvious to me that negative or positive input at the time a child tries to speak or entertain has an equal affect on the success of a similar situation in the future. For human beings to survive there must be events that have the property of reinforcing its behavior. Broadly speaking, the range of effective reinforcement widens. Food can reinforce behavior from the earliest days of life. Visual patterns, like a bottle or rubber spoon, soon come to take on reinforcing properties for the infant. To me, it is most noticeable when a pacifier is in the infant's mouth. I have observed that as soon as something exciting comes into focus, the speed of sucking increases and becomes more forceful. Feeding our triplet grandchildren has enhanced my belief. We line them up to eat and they are like little birds in a nest. Their little mouths open wide each time a spoonful passes them, even if it is going to the next child.

Positive reinforcement can elicit the same increase in emotion in the child. Put a bottle full of milk or juice near them and the rate quickens; turn out the light and leave the room and the same phenomenon happens. The difference…one is positive and the other is negative. As our children grow, we can identify characteristics that give signs that our reinforcement is working. When our children raided the refrigerator, I was sure that the only reinforcement was food. Fortunately, I finally learned that this was erroneous on my part. They actually feel welcome in our home, and that is a good feeling.

Not all children will be like Pavlov's dogs and begin to salivate when some reinforcement is given, but there will be a behavior indicator. With our children, it was generally a smile or perhaps a long face that told us the reaction to the reinforcement.

Learn to Salvage Listening Errors

When our youngest son was four years old, he started playing soccer on an under-six team at the local YMCA program. He was aggressive and quickly became a star on the team. Kevin was able to compete with the five-year-old girls who, at that age, were substantially larger and more agile than the boys. Kevin was quick and displayed no fear, so his coach chose to play him in the goalkeeper position.

One day after one of the first few practices in his new sport, Kevin and I were driving home from practice. I was driving my 1965 Mustang and Kevin was sitting in the backseat. He snuggled up close to me between the seats and proceeded to tell me what a great goaldy (his word) he was. He was explaining how far he could kick the ball, and that the coach said he was the best goaldy on the team…and the story went on-and-on.

For a while, I listened intently, gave positive reinforcement messages, tussled his hair, and even managed a cheek-to-cheek hug. Then the unforgivable occurred. An Eagles song came on the radio. The Eagles were (and still are) my favorite musical group. Do not get me wrong, I cannot blame the band for my actions, but they contributed.

Without thinking, I reached over, turned the radio up louder, and began to sing *Peaceful Easy Feeling* as Kevin was telling me his story. I honestly cannot tell you the events that occurred during the next few minutes because I was so engrossed in personal pleasure. When I finally looked back, Kevin was curled up at the back window looking up at the sky and passing building tops.

Then it hit me. I had made a major "Daddy made a boo boo" type error. All of the positive reinforcement that I had given prior to the time I increased the radio volume had been instantly erased by the one act of negative reinforcement. Instinctively, I knew that there must be some way to fill in the cavernous opening between father and son. I went through the motions of making the car feel like something was happening to the engine by changing the pressure on the gas pedal and ultimately pulling to the side of the road. In a last ditch effort to find forgiveness, I took a chance.

I asked Kevin to stay in the car while I checked under the hood. I removed a wire while going through the motions of looking for the problem. I went back to the car, picked up my little four-year-old, and asked for his help. I told him that I could not find the problem and that I believed he could. After only a few minutes, he noticed the loose spark plug wire. When he pointed it out, I replaced it with his help and returned to the car. When it started almost immediately (I admit to being surprised since it was not the most dependable car anyway), I gave all the positive words I could.

When we got home, I encouraged Kevin to tell his mother about the great day he had at soccer. He also enthusiastically provided input into the fact that Daddy had not found the problem when the car quit working and he had helped fix it.

Many accolades were passed along that evening, and a devastating negative was somewhat salvaged. We believe it worked, because not only is he a good speaker, soccer player, and student, but he can replace whole engines in his own car. I know… because he asks me to hold the light and hand him the tools.

If Schools Don't Teach It...It's Up to You

During formative school years, teachers spend time in the classroom teaching children to read and write. Think back to your own education and try to remember the total number of courses you took that taught those two basic communication skills. Now, try to remember the courses you were required to take that related to speaking in public or, more importantly, listening.

You should be able to count on one hand the total number of speech classes, and I would be shocked if you needed more than one finger to calculate the times you attended a listening class in school. It has always been interesting to me that we were taught to read and write, but school systems tend to ignore the skills we use most often in the communication process. At least that is the way it was for those of us in the baby-boom generation.

Fortunately, we are seeing some efforts to correct that issue in schools all over the country. More speech, drama, interpretive reading, and listening classes are added to the curriculum each year. Nevertheless, the ability (or lack of) to communicate is developed in those early pre-school years where the parent has an enormous influence. Remember my opinion that habits formed by age seven last a lifetime?

Some children in kindergarten and beyond seem to have great difficulty communicating or knowing how to speak. Day-care professionals and elementary teachers are often perplexed by the way some children control the use of vocal cues. Certain children seem to yell all the time when they talk. They do not differentiate talking on the playground from talking in front of the family, a class environment, or their friends in a small group. Others speak softly, and it is difficult to hear them at all.

Obviously, vocal tones, pitch, and volume provide problems for some of these children, and exercises to help them develop control over vocal quality are included in the addendum section.

The language arts textbooks in schools offer suggestions for working with stress, juncture, and pitch in conjunction with reading and language arts activities. Most of these are valuable as the child is led to realize that it is possible to control the voice. Parents have a wide variety of options to use in working to improve the basic vocal quality skills. Some are helpful in teaching manners. My son Brent reminds his children to "use your quiet voice," or "use the restaurant volume, please." I am always amazed at how well it works. Nevertheless, I should not be surprised considering the praise that follows the requested behavior.

Even though there is some tension attached to using a video camera by most adults, children do not experience the same anxiety and apprehension. The camera recording can be a friend and an effective tool to help develop the talents that makes the child a quality speaker.

It is also fun for the child to see their performance, hear the recorded applause, and sense the positive feedback from family during the viewing. Big grins, happy laughter, and more applause go a long way with children. Consider using video when you work with your children on the activities in this book's addendum.

Making the Most of Storytelling

Storytelling has been used extensively in camp programs for scouting and church youth groups for years. History tells us that much of what we know about other civilizations was passed down through the efforts of the storytellers. There is no set time to tell stories, but storytelling around a campfire at night has a magic of its own. Seldom will families have the opportunity to have a campfire, but finding ways to sit in small circles close to each other often has the same effect. We have learned to use our chiminea in the back yard to add some ambiance to storytelling time.

Use the Stories from Everyday Life
In my experience with youth groups, I have learned to use the locale, whether woods, seashore, or mountains, to allow children to repeat stories they know. I have always been interested in astronomy, and a starry night is the perfect time to tell legends of the stars and sky beings. The characters get lost in the mass of stars, but the children do not seem to mind if I cannot quite find Pegasus or Ursa Major when telling the story.

Stories come from everyday events. When we took our children skiing, we were creating stories. My sons were not very old the morning that I woke them early for a trip to the lake before work for me and school for them. We were on the lake at sunrise, each boy had two ski runs, and the day was perfect in every way. When we started back to the boat dock, the boat suddenly died. We were mid lake with no other boaters in sight, and this was long before cell phones. I remember Brent saying, "We are going to be late to school." Then he thanked me. I am not sure what that was all about.

Needless to say, we were all late for our respective obligations that morning. After rowing in to a close shoreline, walking to a house up the hill, calling Mom, towing the boat along the shore, and other fun events, there were plenty of stories.

I still enjoy hearing their version of the morning. It changes over time, but the memories are still there when repeated to family and friends. Making stories means spending time with your children and allowing them to repeat what happened during your outing or excursion.

We have a Magnolia tree in our yard that children love to climb. One of my favorite times is after my four-year-old granddaughter emerges from the tree. I like to ask her what she saw, how cold or hot it was, and what she pretended to be. What a glorious time to talk to the pre-school child and give applause for the story. Of course, we have to tell the story to GiGi as soon as possible.

Choose the Stories Carefully…but Choose

Ghost stories are a favorite, but these are best reserved for telling to older boys and girls. I have learned that younger children enjoy scary stories in more familiar surroundings. On rainy afternoons when your children cannot play outside is a great time to allow for a storytelling event. Invite other children over and let them take turns telling stories indoors. These round robins encourage children to become storytellers. Providing early opportunity to tell stories in comfortable settings with friends and family can help reduce stage fright later in life.

If you have children in the middle and upper grades, you may find that they enjoy telling stories to younger children, and younger children respond enthusiastically. There are many values to be gained, but the most significant is why this book was written. The young storyteller develops confidence in speaking before a group, learns to express thoughts clearly, and comes to appreciate the power of words.

Folklore

Storytelling can be tied in with the study of folklore. Collecting local folklore is a valuable experience for young people.

My ancestors settled in Delaware in the late 17th century. When my brothers, our wives, and I visited Lewes, Delaware, a few years ago, we learned much about our family and the history of the region. People shared what they knew about Lewes during the war of 1812 and even showed us some historical items from our family. The history and stories intrigued me, and I plan to share them with my grandchildren with the expectation that they will be passed to future generations.

I purchased a book titled *Cornstalks and Cannonballs* by Barbara Mitchell. It tells about how the townspeople in Lewes outsmarted the powerful British Navy during the war of 1812. I know that if I could take my grandchildren there, show them the town and the bay, tell the story with enthusiasm because it is about our family heritage, they will be able to tell it their way, and I like that. Because of perception, I expect there will be five different versions of the same story.

The point here is that there are stories in almost any town. Grapevine, Texas, has a steam engine that takes people on sightseeing tours. It provides a taste of the turn of the 20th century and allows parents the opportunity to tell stories that can be repeated by their children in an on-stage setting. Look around your town, take your child to do something fun that he can talk about later. Arrange for family and friends to be an audience so your four-, five-, six-, or seven-year-old child can tell about the train ride, and don't forget the applause.

The desire to tell should come from the child and not be required of the child by you, a teacher, or other adult. Universally liked stories, folktales, and fairy tales that may already be familiar from having heard them told in preschool classes can be great sources to encourage them to speak in public. Old favorites can be checked out at local libraries for you to read to your child. *The Bremen Town Musicians, Cinderella,* and *The Three Wishes* are good choices. There are also some fun short stories for you to read. Be sure to applaud and ask your child or student for a repeat performance when they reenact the story.

Stories lasting from five to ten minutes are long enough for the young storyteller. Because many children speak rapidly, you may have to emphasize that a story must be told slowly enough for the listeners to follow the storyline. Children learning to be storytellers should have an opportunity to hear stories told by more than one adult so that they become aware of different styles of telling. Through observation, they will pick up many techniques for good storytelling.

Picture Book Stories

You may start the children with picture-book-storytelling. Give him practice in holding the book so everyone can see the pictures as he tells the story. Children retain much more than we think about stories you have read to them. If he does not get the story exactly right when telling it from the pictures only, do not correct him. Give the applause and read it again later. When a new audience appears, ask him to tell the story again. Eventually, it is repeated very close to what they hear from you. Use vocal fluctuation and different voices to make it more interesting. You will probably begin to hear your vocal tone when he tells it.

What Is Available in Your Town?

Some communities have Storyteller Guilds. Your local library may have storytelling special events. Check it out and get you and your child involved. Know in advance the stories your child plans to tell. Have the books on hand from which the stories are taken. If the storyteller forgets the story, the rest of it can be read from the book, and she will pick up where she remembers the storyline. It is okay to share the responsibility; just do not take over and leave her out.

Family story hours are much like game night. This type of program is usually planned for early evening, about 7:30 or 8:00 p.m., so that the family has time to complete dinner and children settle in from play. The family hour should be planned for any age children, but we found that if you have different age groups in your family, story hour should begin early for toddlers. Let them hear brothers and sisters and you tell stories. Let them share if they want to, and you will find that storytelling will last well into the elementary school years. Oh yes, did I mention, do not forget the applause?

In addition, if you have children of different ages, infant to elementary, it may be best to isolate this time for the older children to give them the feeling of importance. It is evident that you may find it difficult to separate the age groups, but there is some merit to spending quality time with each rather than together. This may also be an opportune time for parents, grandparents, neighbors, or older children to participate in the storytelling. It is okay for the younger children to be taken aside for a picture-book hour.

About forty minutes should be allocated for the actual storytelling. Stories, poetry, and music suitable for the older group should be presented. There are children's songs on CD and on dish and network music programs that could even be playing in the background while the story is being told.

I am convinced that telling stories for family and friendly audiences can be beneficial to children as they grow. One student shared this memory from his past, and I believe it crystallizes this belief.

> A positive memory I have about public speaking is when I stood at the front of a tour bus when I was nine and recited Jeff Foxworthy jokes for all of two hours in front of my family and around forty strangers. That day is one of my happiest memories, and I loved the applause.
>
> Oliver

Use Your Libraries

Family Evening Story Hours in the libraries often bring adults and college-age students to provide entertainment for you and your child. In speaking of the values of these story hours, parents often experience a new relationship with their children. It becomes an emotional bond that finds release in shared laughter, shared adventure, and shared confidences. Children experience a new understanding of their parents' concerns, learn from other storytellers, and perhaps begin to mimic the storytelling techniques they observe. The important thing is that together, you and your child enjoy a storyteller's art.

Use Stories to Simplify

For as long as I can remember, I have been fascinated by stories; I have been especially fond of Cajun stories. The Cajun Chef, Justin Wilson, was on television each day when the school bus delivered me to the stop across the tracks from our home. I preferred watching him to cartoons, but he took second place to my favorite horse shows, *Fury* and *My Friend Flicka.* I learned to mimic his dialect and repeat the stories he told during his cooking program. When friends came to our house, my mother would call me in from outside and suggest that it was time to hear a few Cajun stories. Everyone always laughed and made positive comments, and the truth of the matter is, like "Pistol" Pete Maravich in basketball, I do not ever remember failing as a speaker. My audience was set up to be the most supportive you can imagine.

It is these same types of effort that can help parents nurture the skills and talents in their children. Remember, these are skills that will go away or be negatively effected if parents demonstrate their own personal fear of speaking. It is the positive skills that will become a significant part of the child's future if they feel comfortable speaking and have, with your help, avoided hearing the negative comments.

Combating Negatives

Unfortunately, the older a child grows, the more he or she is influenced by the negative input of parents, teachers, or peers. Although they are meant to be examples of basic courtesy and manners, phrases like "Don't talk when grown-ups are talking," or, "It's not nice to be loud around other people," can influence a child to worry about speaking in public. A teacher might say. "If you talk without raising your hand, you'll be sent to the principal's office," and, of course, the most damaging negative feedback comes from sources the parents have no control over or seldom even know about…peers.

Slowly, but surely, the negative comments, giggles, and snickers of peers and/or the big people in a child's life have an effect on the way they think, speak, and feel. Children internalize a myth early that they are incapable of communicating with the spoken word.

The Student Who Got My Attention
Having taught speech for several years at the college level, I have witnessed varied reactions to the fear of public speaking. Remember the opening paragraph in Chapter One. The college freshman came to me early in the semester to say that he would not be able to give a speech. I said, "You have to, it's a speech class."

The student informed me that he would be much too afraid to speak in front of the class and begged to be relieved of the responsibility. I told him that was not an option. "This is a speech class," I repeated. After much discussion regarding course requirements, we agreed that he would write a speech in manuscript that he could read to the class rather than deliver in the required extemporaneous presentation style.

He stopped by my office periodically during the next few weeks to review the material he was writing and gather opinions and positive strokes. Obviously, he had cause to believe he would never be a speaker and should stay off the platform. Together, we wrote a very informative, high-energy speech. He seemed excited and, after a few actual readings one-on-one in the office, he appeared relaxed enough to deliver the assigned speech in class.

The night finally came when he would be called on to make the presentation to the class. When asked if he was ready to motivate and inform his fellow students, his response was, "I'll probably pass out!" And so he did!

When his name was announced, he quietly rose from his desk holding that wonderful speech in white-knuckled hands. He had a distant gaze fixed on the neatly typed pages as he moved from his desk to the podium. He faced the class. In the presence of that menacing silence that can only be heard when the audience senses something grave is about to happen, he started reading the speech.

My heart leapt with pride. *He is going to make it,* I thought. My coaching was about to be a proven success. Suddenly, he made a terrible mistake...he looked up! When his eyes met others in the audience, his face turned the snow-white color of the paper he was holding. His eyes rolled back in his head, and he passed out. Talk about a self-fulfilling prophecy!

After some nervous moments and compresses to stop the bleeding, he came to. Another student took him to the school emergency room to have the gash above his eye sewn together.

It was not until the following week that we learned it took twelve stitches to sew the laceration caused by the impact of his forehead against the corner of a classroom desktop.

Those same twelve stitches may have been the source that turned his speaking career around and helped him develop a renewed self-confidence.

The next time I saw him was two weeks later. He came to the classroom, took his seat, and listened intently to the lecture. After class, he came to me and said, "I really need to talk to you." I immediately apologized for forcing him to do something he so vehemently did not want to do. He waved off my comment and said, "You don't know what I plan to do with my life, do you?"

"No," I replied. Then I waited patiently to hear what this young man planned to do without the ability to speak in public. Programmer, perhaps? Anything but a career that included speaking to an audience.

He said, "I'm going to be a preacher." I know I must have had some awful expression of disbelief and doubt. He simply said, "Thank you for helping me realize that I have to face my fear." I said, "You are welcome. Now what?"

I helped him find professional help, and after graduation, he went to a seminary and now ministers at a small church in his hometown. It is easy to envision his fear every time he stands before an audience, but he has learned to make the butterflies in his stomach soar in confident formation.

Regrettably, someone had taught this young man the myth that speaking can be hazardous to his health…and he believed. It was only through dogged determination and positive strokes from people who cared about his future that he unlearned the myth and relearned that he was a capable speaker.

My student who refused to speak in a speech class had heard the myth all his life. It ended with twelve stitches. Perhaps we can learn and teach a little less dramatically.

The event caused me to look inwardly to find what it was that gave me the courage and outright desire to be a public speaker.

Letting Go

And a woman who held a babe against her bosom said, Speak to us of Children.

And he said:

Your children are not your children.

They are the sons and daughters of Life's longing for itself.

They come through you but not from you,

And though they are with you yet they belong not to you.

You may give them your love but not your thoughts.

For they have their own thoughts.

You may house their bodies but not their souls,

For their souls dwell in the house of tomorrow, which you cannot visit, not even in your dreams.

You may strive to be like them, but seek not to make them like you.

For life goes not backward nor tarries with yesterday.

You are the bows from which your children as living arrows are sent forth.

The archer sees the mark upon the path of the infinite, and He bends you with His might that His arrows may go swift and far.

Let your bending in the archers hand be for gladness;

For even as he loves the arrow that flies, so

He loves also the bow that is stable.[1]

Kahlil Gibran

This saying from Kahlil Gibran's *The Prophet* emphasizes the point that parents are not the controlling factor in their children's lives. The analogy of parents being a bow that puts the arrow, the child, on the path leads me to this section on letting go. The more stable the parent, the more likely the arrow will fly straight and the child's self-esteem will develop. There are so many ways a parent can help or hinder a child's self-esteem. I believe that one of the best positive approaches is controlled letting go.

When my first child was born, I spent several hours by the crib just watching him, admiring him, and I remember thinking how helpless he was. It also crossed my mind that I would someday have to let go and allow him to venture out on his own. Brent seemed completely dependent on me to keep him alive and healthy. There was some pressure inside me to make decisions for him. I felt that I would be making them all his life. I quickly learned my beliefs were far from the truth.

Be Aware of the Natural Instincts

Our boys, as are all children, were surprisingly aware of the world around them. It became apparent through their growth that they were born with a variety of natural instincts to help them survive. Those natural tendencies are nature's way of helping them grow and become contributors to society. With this in mind, it is important for parents to *let go* and let nature and the child work together to create a healthy, confident child. So how do we get to the letting-go stage without the risk of pushing a child into something that may be dangerous or detrimental to self-esteem? I felt it was important to discuss successes with parent to see how they had directed their children's lives and managed the concept of letting go.

In one session with parents of teenage children, they were asked why their teenagers were achieving different successes in school, church, home, and other environments.

One mother said that her personal goals had always been to be a model and actor. For various reasons, she had never achieved that objective. As many parents do, she chose to live vicariously through her daughter. She told the group, "Before Agatha was born I made special efforts to sing to her every day. I played music on the stereo that emphasized the natural beauty of the human voice."

After the birth, she continued to sing to the infant, helped her learn songs as she grew, and even played musical games in the car as they traveled. The effort has every appearance of paying off. Aggie has a beautiful voice and is confident in her ability to perform.

On the other hand, Travis' mother, in the same meeting, explained to the group that her son has a magnificent voice, is enrolled in professional voice-training schools, and has demonstrated confidence in his ability to perform before audiences.

She noted that she "can't carry a tune in a paper bag, and seldom listen to music on the radio."

No one can tell us why there are differences in the response children have to early, even prenatal training, but we do know that children are born with abilities, and parents have significant influence on how the talents develop. We do not make children what they are, but we make it possible for them to become what they are meant to be.

The mother who sang to and with her daughter gave specific training to influence behaviors, while the mother who had no skills to help train simply supported and encouraged her son to become what he wanted. It will be interesting to check the progress as the two continue to grow and mature into their place in life.

You also play a vital role in the way your children develop right from the start. Your style of parenting, the choices you make, and the training you give lends support to the future of each child.

Encourage Independence

Letting go is often thought of as the time when a child leaves for college or gets married. We should all remember that the desire for independence develops early. The toddler asserts, "Me do it!" Shoes may be on opposite feet, but the action to put them on belongs to the child. Children are pleased with themselves when they meet new challenges and experience success in any task.

A child learns to excel at a task by doing it repeatedly. This experience is important to their learning process. By allowing the child to try new tasks rather than believing they are too young may result in successful completion of tasks. It becomes a building block for feelings of positive self-worth.

People who have learned to speak in public or perform on stage did not develop the skill overnight. It developed slowly. Confidence and self-reliance take time. The ability to know when to provide support and when to refrain from interference is an integral part of parenting toward these skills.

In a variety of ways, parents can discourage a child's efforts. A child may want to tie his or her shoes, but the parent does not feel there is enough time to allow the unskilled hands to attempt the task. Because the parent wants to be needed, they do not want to give up control.

I believe that parents lose the opportunity to teach important skills and prevent the child from strengthening self-esteem when the child is discouraged from trying to complete a task on his own. Encourage the child to try new skills, practice them, and learn how to function independently and with confidence.

Recognize and Praise Successes

Experiencing success is an important part of moving toward self-reliance. Children feel successful when parents recognize and praise their efforts and accomplishments. Refrain from criticizing less-than-perfect results when children are excited about doing a task. Avoid showing a better way until later. Allow the thrill of accomplishment to be enjoyed.

> I believe that my fear of public speaking corresponds with how I was raised. My grandparents felt that children should never have a voice in a "grown folk's" conversation. My mother never let me speak for myself when asked a question because she felt that I would leave out some vital information or that I wouldn't be able to verbalize what her response would be. So she spoke for me before I could open my mouth. Now I'm an adult and still find it difficult

to speak in most situations. But my friends are a big help; they encourage me to speak in groups and seem to genuinely be interested in my opinion.

Dawnyale

Negative Comments Hurt

To help a child become independent, it is helpful to stick with positive comments about the child's efforts and accomplishments. The motivation to try again is often destroyed by negative criticisms. Often parents do not even realize the comments they make are negative.

I recently counseled a woman who had no children of her own but married a father of two very intelligent young boys. At the time of our conversation, the ages were eleven and twelve. Her complaint was regarding the lack of homework production. She told me that she and her husband had informed their older son (who, by the way, had been diagnosed as having ADD) that because he could not get his homework done, he could not watch television or use his computer. Her often-repeated words, "You can't get your homework done, so you can't watch TV or play at your computer," were negative and a problem. The difficulty came from the words, "You can't."

Try New Approaches

I asked her to change the approach and say, "You are so smart. I really like it when you get your homework done so we will have some time to play at your computer later this evening." There will be no way of knowing whether she tries the new approach, but I firmly believe that his behavior will modify when he is not personally attacked and only his behaviors are evaluated.

So When Do You Let Go?

My wife and I often discussed when the time would be right to let go and allow our sons to handle their own food in public, select clothing, drive, and eventually to choose their life mates. The key had to do with their personal readiness. *Is the child ready to do what he or she wants to try? Is the child ready for what the parent is insisting that the child do?* Some children are not ready for certain kinds of independence, even when children think they are or when their parents wish they would be ready.

We believed that our children would be harmed if we expected maturity beyond their abilities. Impractical expectations harm self-esteem and the child's ability to become self-reliant.

I am equally concerned that underestimating a child's abilities and expecting too little can also reduce a child's self-confidence and make the child unwilling to do things for him or herself. When parents delay opportunities for demonstrating self-reliance, they run the risk of reducing a child's capabilities and make the child further dependent or rebellious.

Talk about the Can Do, not the Can't Do

How often have your heard or perhaps said, "Oh, he's just not ready to play a rough sport," or, "She's too young to learn how to use a computer"? The sad reality here is that the child hears the message and often internalizes it as true if repeated often enough.

It is never too early to teach a child the basic skill of responsibly calling 911, or repeating their home address to a police officer, or finding an escape route in case of fire. When those tasks are performed correctly, the appropriate affirmations will help solidify the retention of the skill.

Judging Readiness

The question parents must ask is, "How do we judge readiness?" Parents must be aware of child development and be attentive to the way children develop capabilities. Pay attention to the child's desire to learn how to do a new task. Our children begged to drive from the time they could talk. Since I was a young driver on the farm, it was tempting. Even though my parents started letting me drive in the country when I was eight and allowed me to drive my mother to Colorado from Texas when I was eleven, my wife just would not allow it for our sons.

My parents demonstrated support when I needed to move toward self-reliance and independence. The release my parents gave me was not sound or logical. Fortunately, I, nor my family or others on the road were harmed by the actions, and my self-confidence was definitely bolstered, but it was dangerous, not sound or logical.

Besides allowing the child to try new experiences, a parent can teach needed skills or arrange for the child to learn them, provide encouragement, and let the child know that it is okay to make mistakes. Being present for the new events in the child's life is important. However, parents cannot be physically present at all times. Through modern technology, they can be emotionally available to the child. It is comforting to a child to hear, "You can call me at the office, in my car, or on my way to the corporate office in Torrance, California." While the conversation is progressing, the parent can offer all the praise without being physically there.

Letting go means you are coming to terms with both the strengths and limitations of your child, regardless of the child's age. We know that letting go can involve consequences. In some instances, the consequences can be of a great magnitude. Parents want to protect the child, solve his or her problems, be in control, and feel needed. Because of those needs, it is difficult not to do it for them. To let them grow by experience and alone is painful to doting parents. Like it or not, allowing freedom to learn is imperative.

Base It on the Child's Need

Positive letting go is based on the child's need. Letting go that places a parent's needs above the child's needs is potentially damaging to the child's self-esteem. Children can be harmed physically and emotionally when they are expected to be independent and self-reliant before they have the skills. To force a child to speak in public can easily cause the fear they ultimately experience as adults. One student answered a survey question regarding the reason for personal speech anxiety. Her answer, "I was forced to publicly tell people in my parent's Church about the bad things I did during the week. I always remember that."

When a parent gives up appropriate responsibility and forces the child into too much self-reliance, the child may feel neglected.

Allow the Child to Take Responsibility

Sometimes parents need to step back and allow the child to take responsibility. Instead of trying to control the child, the parent can make the child responsible for certain problems. When a parent allows the child to be responsible for decisions and mistakes, the child can feel pride in making good decisions and the child can learn from mistakes, especially when mistakes are seen as a natural part of learning.

When our children asked the "What do you want me to do with this, Daddy?" question, we let them make a personal choice by saying, "Where do you (with emphasis on you) think it should be?" Amazingly enough, they generally made the right decisions. We gave appropriate praise for the correct decisions and did not have to help them make similar decisions in the future.

If parents make it clear that it is acceptable to make mistakes, children are more willing to experience something new. Parents can say in words and show by their actions that mistakes are to be expected when persons try something new. Children should understand that they are loved, whether or not they make mistakes.

Trusting a child to be capable and allowing him or her opportunity to make mistakes and learn from them is both respectful and caring. It gives the child confidence and prevents them from being programmed to do nothing by a parent who does too much.

Be Aware of Personal Emotions

Letting go usually involves a variety of emotional experiences for parents. Self-reliance may represent ends to certain stages in a parent's life as well as the child's. A parent may see growing independence as loss of control over children and their lives, a realization that the parent is no longer needed in quite the same way as before. Parents may begin to feel left out, and worse, getting old. On the other hand, a parent can find it exciting to watch children face challenges and tackle them successfully.

When a child experiences a new and significant event, it can be frightening. The child may appear brave and daring one day and want to be protected and cared for the next. Messages to children are often mixed. We may want our children to make their own decisions, but we want them to decide to do what we think is best. We may want children to use their judgment, but we want them to follow our advice.

When Feelings Are Out of Balance

It is helpful to both the child and the parent when the parent can recognize out-of-balance feelings. Then the parent can send fewer mixed messages. Saying things like, "Go outside to play, but don't get dirty," is a contradiction in the child's mind and may prove to be too much pressure for them. Parents may find it beneficial to talk with one another about their mixed feelings.

When children are well prepared for independence and self-reliance, parents can feel more confident about letting them go experience life on their own. Regrettably, the American society as a whole is letting go of children more and more without providing proper support.

Very young children are being left alone with no supervision because childcare is expensive and may be unavailable. Some or all these cases may be somebody else's children. Yet these situations touch all our lives.

If they are not your own children, they may be the ones next door, down the block, at school with your children, or in another town and state, but what happens to these children affects our children and us. Extra taxes, crime, disrupted classrooms where learning cannot take place, or unwholesome influences on our children are only some of the results.

The following quote from a student shows that it may not be in our families that we are experiencing certain situations, but in friends' or other family members' families. Even though the Alyson was not experiencing it firsthand, she was still effected by her friend.

> My best friend's parents divorced when she was young. She lived mostly with her mother, who worked during the day. There were a lot of days where she had to be alone at

home. She said she was very outgoing before the divorce, but she is very shy now and is afraid to speak in public. I don't have a fear, and I believe it is because my parents were always available and encouraged me to tell my stories. I didn't have to be alone. I think I would have been different if I had to be alone more.

Alyson

I do not expect the social problems to be solved by people who read this book. The reality is that you and I cannot reach out to every broken child who comes along. We can, however, influence our own families and trust them to spread the message to their children, neighbors, friends, and the occasional person who simply observes a caring behavior.

Parents who are available for quality time with children can influence them in a positive manner. The following chapter provides some ideas for giving children special time. I believe it can make a difference in both children and parents.

Quality Time

Looking back over my life as a father, I can tell you that the thousands of hours spent with our children are invaluable to my wife and me. The time spent playing, talking, and including their friends in family activities has returned unimaginable joy and benefit to our lives and, I believe, to the lives of our sons.

Our sons' lives as children and now as adults have proven that the investment was worth every moment. If you were to ask me now what I would do differently as a parent, I would tell you that I would spend more time with my children. Although I remember those years between seven and thirteen when I thought I could easily trade them for several weeks of solitary confinement and come out ahead, I can never forget the teenage years that brought us so close together.

We bought a boat when our sons were ten and eleven years old. We taught them to ski, trusted them with the wheel of the boat (with a watchful eye of course), encouraged friends to join us on the water, and took them on outings even when we thought we were just too pooped. I shall always believe that the time granted has rewarded our family with two very mannerly, intelligent, and socially acceptable young men.

Granted, mistakes were made. You will know by your own experience that no family is perfect, and I do not claim to be an exception. The key to our success, however, was the desire of my wife and me to set aside time to spend with the boys. Both are very articulate and more than willing to speak in public and impress their audiences. Their success did not come from ignoring the seemingly meaningless banter of a toddler or the late-night bedside chats about friends, soccer, and automobiles.

Quality Time Pays Off

The quality of the time granted has proven successful for our family, and I am convinced it pays off for all families. There is no way you can sit down with your child and say, "Okay, let's have thirty minutes of quality time." The words themselves set limits on the time together and imply a command rather than a desire to really communicate and have fun learning.

The quality-time issue has been debated for years by behaviorists. The questions asked are, "How long should it be?" "Where should the time be spent?" "Should there be one-on-one time?" and so on.

In my mind, quality time is tremendously important. It could be planned days for specific occasions. I intentionally spent individual time with my sons on their birthdays, usually followed their suggestions, and together we planned trips to historic places in the local community, to zoos, to museums, or to other family members' homes. The times I remember best were when all of us just lay in the grass on a moonless night watching for meteors and man-made satellites and pointing out planets.

There was an evening in the mountains where we were up late enough to watch the moon set and Jupiter rise within thirty minutes of each event. What a special occasion that was. I could share my love of the universe, teach a little about the solar system, and spend time with my sons. For me, it did not get much better than that. I doubt that they were quite as pleased by the stargazing as I, but they asked lots of questions and made me feel great.

Be Specific about the Amount of Time

Seldom is quality time significant if it is time set aside so that you can spend thirty minutes with your child with the attitude, "Okay, we have thirty minutes. What do you want to tell me?" The truly important time is when you plan to spend an evening together that includes a little yard work, washing the family car, or any together task that can be followed by some time in the kitchen dreaming up some exotic, never-before-heard-of-dinner that is just for them.

At times like these, you can easily transition to the activities that will be beneficial to your child's public speaking confidence. I always enjoyed reading Bible stories or a C. S. Lewis chronicle to my sons as youngsters and welcomed the readings they shared from children's books or school literature books. The key was when they wanted to share, to listen and acknowledge their accomplishments.

The games, skits, and activities in this book are designed to allow you to introduce an idea during the fun times. Once they are underway, the support and acknowledgment of their success will get easier each time.

Drama as a Speaking Tool

Drama is an important means of stimulating creativity in problem solving. Drama comes in the form of puppetry, short skits, or creatively acting scenes from imagination. It can challenge a child's view about their world and about themselves. Drama provides students with an outlet for emotions, thoughts, and dreams that they might not otherwise have means to express.

Through drama, a child can become another person, an object, a character in history, or an imagined animal or super hero for just a few moments in time. It helps them face an audience in a safe atmosphere, where actions and consequences can be examined, discussed, and experienced without putting them in a threatening environment. I believe this may be the most important reason for encouraging your children to experience drama. There are a number of drama organizations in most communities. A quick online search can lead most parents to a children's theater group. Interview the leaders to be certain their students are given opportunity to experience all elements of the theater. Ask about their methods of dealing with children. Be comfortable with the answers or go to another. If you are really energetic, start one for your neighborhood.

At the center of all drama is communication. Like all art forms, drama allows children to communicate with and understand others in new ways. Perhaps more than any other art form, drama provides training in the very practical elements of communication children will face in a growing, information-centered world. Children who have participated in dramatic activities are less likely to have difficulty speaking to audiences. They are likely to be more persuasive in their communications, both written and oral.

When my son Brent asked me if there were courses he should take to help him become a better speaker, I suggested that he check into the drama department in his high school and college. He did, and I believe the experience has been positive for him. His confidence as a teacher, leader, and now financial planning professional are evidence.

I also believe that fear of speaking happens long before the advanced education years. With that in mind, this book is focused on children under the age of seven. Drama for preschool age children may feel complicated, but it helps create a more confident self-image early in life. Participation in dramatic activity requires self-control and discipline that will serve the child well in all aspects of life.

An element of drama that is most encouraging to me is that children learn to cooperate and work together with their peers. They learn to find the best way for each child to contribute and to listen to and accept other people's ideas. I do not know of any art form that is more collaborative. Drama is an important tool for preparing young people to live and work in higher education and professional environments that are increasingly team focused. A student shared her feelings about being in a church play. Her enthusiasm emphasizes the importance of drama to build confidence.

> A positive memory I have is when I was a character in a church play. I loved giving my lines and seeing the reaction of the audience once I was through.
>
> Alyson

Drama teaches children to be more tolerant of others. It helps them walk in another's shoes for a brief time. It is evident from watching local news that we live in an intolerant culture; the ability to understand others' motives is critical. Drama can help build responsible adults from the formative pre-school years. A non-threatening event can be experienced with parents and teachers.

There is little that feels better to a parent than to have practiced lines in the family den and finally see them flawlessly delivered on stage. Lead the applause when each act is over. Be proud…it's okay!

Activities Addendum

Because most of out traits, habits, fears, and beliefs have happened before the age of seven, I recommend starting these games between the ages of two and seven. The younger children may need a little time to begin to be involved. Do not rush them; the time will come for them to shine. Some children may be precocious enough to play at two or three, but your child or student will appreciate your patience and feel less pressured.

I divided the activities into two age groups. First, the two- to four-year-olds followed by activities for ages five, six, and seven. If possible, have family members, friends, and/or neighbors gather to be the audience.

Important to know: If you need to lead the child to start talking, questions are generally the best way to get going. The problem is that most people ask yes or no questions. Regrettably, the only response is yes or no. It is imperative that the questions ask for a response that is descriptive or action-oriented. Do not say, "Does your dolly have a name?" Of course, the answer is yes. Instead, say, "Tell me why you named your dolly Samantha." Follow up with, "Great, what does Samantha like to do when you and her play?"

Rather than say, "Is that your soccer ball?" Say, "Tell me how you and Philip play with the soccer ball?" Follow up with, "Wonderful, tell me how you score a goal?" Follow up again with, "Remember when we went to see Uncle Brent's soccer game? Can you tell me about the game and about how he played?"

When the questions are open-ended, there is room to respond. It may require several open-ended questions, but patience generally wins and the child will tell you more and more about the toy, activity, or event.

Activities for Ages Two, Three, and Four

Introducing Daddy by Description
Dad should start by sitting next to the child and doing the introduction.

Say: "This is Abigail. She has long, blonde hair and a big smile. She makes me happy when she sings her special song. Her puppy's name is Hershey, and Abigail likes to play with her. She loves to dress up in her princess dress with fancy shoes. Abigail is such a good big sister. She loves to play with Hannah. Today she is very happy. She makes me happy too."

Dad should then allow the child to introduce him by description.

If she cannot get started, ask her some questions.

"What do you like to do with Daddy?" "What does Daddy do when he is working?" "When Daddy works in the yard, what do you like to help him do?" "What does Daddy's favorite chair look like?" "Tell us about Daddy when he drives."

I hope that these questions will lead to new ideas that will simply start the child talking. Feel free to change the subject to Mommy, a sibling, or a pet.

Remember to applaud.

Act the Parts in a Familiar Book

This is a great exercise. Mom or Dad can be first, but always give the child the opportunity to be the actor. If there is some reluctance from the child to perform, you go first. Generally, the child will be happy to act after a parent demonstrates. Some personalities will always want to be first, but I like to have Mom and Dad act also. Remember, lose your inhibitions.

Read a page in a children's book. When the reading is complete, pretend to be the character that was on the page. Dr. Seuss characters always work well for this exercise.

Paraphrase after reading the lines. "I would not like Green Eggs and Ham anywhere." Add the facial expressions to match the words in each line.

Allow the child to repeat the lines. He or she will usually repeat similar to how they were read. Encourage body motions, facial expression, and tone of voice when they speak.

Remember to applaud.

Play Waiter

Set the stage so that you have a small table with toy plates, cups, saucers, and eating utensils. Help the child determine if he or she wants to be the waiter, or you assume the role.

If you are the diner, say, "Oh, waiter, I would like to have a hamburger, please." Encourage the child to ask what you would like on it. If they will not ask, tell what you want and ask the child to pretend they are making the hamburger.

Typically, the pretend food will be delivered. Be pleased and say, "This looks so good, how did you make it?" Be patient, it may take a short time to assimilate the thoughts, but they will come.

This game can go on for a long time with parent and child reversing roles. I recommend pretending there is food and drink. It can be a messy exercise otherwise.

Remember to applaud.

Let's Go Grocery Shopping

Place some canned goods that are easily recognizable. Spend a little time showing the child that the picture of corn on the label means there is corn inside. If you have time, use plastic cups with pictures of products glued or taped on the side. I like to put the products in different places in the room but close to the stage area so there is action in retrieving.

Parents can pretend to be a shopper. Say, "Oh my, I really need some corn and I can't find it. Can you help me?" When they go retrieve the can, say, "Is this very good corn? Can you tell me how to cook it?"

Let the child describe the product and perhaps pretend to open the can, pour the contents into a microwavable dish, and pretend to cook it. Remember this is just acting, and if it is not the perfect way to cook, it is okay.

Reverse roles and go through all the motions of cooking while asking the child questions, like, "Would you like some pepper on the beans?" or "How about some butter on the asparagus?" Be patient and let the child tell you why he or she likes or dislikes the idea.

Remember to applaud.

Let's Buy some Clothes

Take out some of your shoes, gloves, jackets, and jewelry. Place them on a table that the child can easily reach. Keep the piles neat and begin the exercise by saying, "I want to buy some clothes. Will you help me?"

I like to say, "I want to see the shoes or gloves on someone before I buy. Will you put them on so I can see?" Generally, the jewelry or shoes work best for them to model for you. Alternatively ask, "Will you help me put them on so I can know how they will look on me?" Make a big deal of the style show. Ask them to explain why they think the shoes look good on Mommy or Daddy.

It is easy to reverse the roles. Simply ask them what they want to buy. Ask if they want you to model for them or help them try on the product.

I think it is good to introduce the concept of spending money. If you are the buyer, I recommend you write the child a check, use pretend money (usually cut up pieces of newspaper), or let the child pretend to run a credit card. Be sure to ask how much the product costs. The amount is not relevant, but it is okay to act surprised and ask why they think the product costs so much.

You will want to demonstrate the purchase transactions so they have an idea of what to do. There is nothing like preparing early to teach about money. Sometimes I use real coins and say, "Why don't we put the left over money in savings?" A piggy bank is always a good thing to have around the play area.

Remember to applaud.

Meet My Pet

If you own a pet, this is a good exercise to get the child talking. In addition to the pet, have the collar, leash, food dish, pet food, water bowl, and any other item that is readily related to the animal.

Ask the child to introduce the pet to the audience. Ask him or her to tell how each item is used to make the pet happy. They may demonstrate putting on the collar and attaching the leash. Ask the child to tell what happens when the collar and leash are on. They may tell where they walk, how far, or when.

If the pet is cooperative, allow the child to demonstrate tricks or special ways of petting the pet. Be sure to ask them why they like to play with the pet.

Remember to applaud.

Bus Driver

This is a great activity for family and friends. Arrange chairs so the child is at the front in the driver's seat. Other people should be seated behind the child. I like to put pictures of grandparents, family members, family pets, vacation spots, etc., on a table by the child. Projected pictures on a screen in front of the child are also good. Either way, someone should change the pictures so the child can give a guided tour.

A rider should say, "Oh, bus driver, I would like to go to Grandpa and Grandma's house. Can you drive us there?" Let the child pretend to drive for a few seconds, show a picture, and allow the child to tell the riders about his or her grandparents. If the child has been to an amusement park and there are pictures, a rider should say, "Oh, bus driver, I would like to go to the park. Can you take us there?"

Let the child take the riders on a tour of the park via his or her imagination and memory. Oohs and ahhs are appropriate during the tour.

This exercise can have roles reversed as well. You may have to use quick imagination if the child asks to go somewhere and you have no pictures. It is okay to lose your inhibitions.

Remember to applaud.

Show and Tell

This is one of the easier exercises to get a child performing. Allow them to pick out some of their favorite toys, pictures of family members, or pets as the impetus for show and tell.

I like to have four of five items on a small table. Ask the child to pick an item and tell his or her audience about it. If they pick up a toy and cannot seem to get started talking about it, the time for questions has arrived. For example, if it is a doll, say, "What a beautiful doll. How do you play with her?" "Can you tell me what she likes to do when she plays with you?"

This activity has worked in school classrooms for years, and it can be a big hit at home as well.

Remember to applaud.

Prop Box

Put some of Mommy and Daddy's clothing, hats, jewelry, etc., in a box. Let the child pick something from the prop box and have them act like the person to whom the prop belongs. You will want to demonstrate this.

For example, Daddy may take out one of Mom's scarves. He can hold it and act something that the child will know is what Mommy does. For example, if she always sings while she is preparing a meal, the dad can pretend to cook and sing the song Mommy generally sings.

If Mom takes Dad's baseball cap out of the prop box, she may want to pretend to start a lawnmower and mow the carpet. She may even stop the pretend mower and make believe she is talking to a neighbor across the fence, just as Daddy does.

This can be little tricky for this age bracket, but I have found that the children have a good idea about how their parents act. Do not push the younger ones, and feel free to move the exercise to older age groups.

It works well and can be a great way for the child to earn some applause for his or her acting ability.

Remember to applaud.

Activities for Ages Five, Six, and Seven

Speaking Sounds and Volume Development

This age group is beginning to develop characteristics that will remain with them for a lifetime. They experiment with their voice and even try different dialects. They may pretend to talk like someone they hear on a TV program or a neighbor who has a unique sound to their voice. It is a good part of their development, and the following exercises allow the child to be on stage while experimenting more with their voices.

Parents spend time teaching their children to read and identify objects to get them ready for school days, but some children seem to have great difficulty communicating or knowing how to talk and read aside from the actual words. Some of this difficulty can be removed by enabling the child to control the use of tone and volume. Language arts textbooks offer suggestions for working with stress, juncture, and pitch in conjunction with reading and speaking activities. These are quite valuable tools if the child is led to realize that it is possible to control these things by controlling the voice. For teachers in classrooms or parents in playgroups, the range of possible exercises widens. Tape recorders are encouraged in these exercises. All children should have an opportunity to hear how they sound in different talking situations. They should also experiment with voice volume, pitch, mood, rate, and quality.

These games can be played in classroom settings for school exercises, or they can be played in small groups with friends. Most planned playgroups meet one or two times per week.

If those groups schedule thirty minutes to play one of these games, children will benefit and have opportunity to enhance speaking skills.

A mom, dad, teacher, or whoever is leading should also play the game. Set the example so the child has some idea of expectations.

Changing My Voice

Select one child from the playgroup to sit in a chair or desk facing away from the others. Blindfold or have his or her eyes hidden so the child cannot see the other children or their approach from behind. Take turns pointing to different children in the class who should then walk up behind the desk or chair and knock on it. The child in the chair should say, "Who's there?" and the child who knocked, using an unusual voice, answers by saying *Bibby Brown* (or any other creative name you can imagine).

The child in the chair should then get two chances to guess who the person really is; if the child succeeds, he or she gets to remain in the chair, but if not, the person who knocked gets to take a turn in the chair. This game can be played under a variety of conditions, such as the following: (1) all children must use their normal voices; (2) all children must disguise their voices; (3) all children must use their highest-pitched voice; (4) all children must use their deepest voice; or (5) all children may free-form their voices (i.e., use any pitch, tone, and so forth that they want).

Parents or teachers may want demonstrate by knocking and answering in a high-pitched childlike voice. You should get lots of laughter from very enthusiastic youngsters.

Applause!

Voice Emotions

Explain to the children that they are going to play a game in which they will be talking loudly and softly and in many different manners. They are going to try to express to the others a variety of emotions, such as excited, happy, sad, or scared. Depending on the age group, you can ask them to demonstrate joy, sorrow, reverence, and love. They are not going to be able to tell the others about it but must get it across in one of the following ways:

- By counting from 1 to 10
- By saying "La la la la la la la la"
- By saying only the words "Bang, bang, bang . . ."
- By saying only the words "Sleep, sleep, sleep . . ."
- You can make up words or use familiar names to demonstrate the emotion.

The child who is doing the talking should be behind some sort of screen or turn to the wall so that facial expressions cannot be seen by the other students. The other children, as well as family members, or friends and neighbors can also guess the emotion. Lots of praise helps the child know their voice, tone, and volume helps others know how they feel.

Applause!

Scary Voice Contest
Or a variation...Friendly Voice Contest

Have the children organize and conduct a scary voice contest. Let the playgroup and parents act as judges. Work out ahead of time the criterion for judging and some general rules or guidelines so that all judges and contestants will know what they are looking for. In the end, everyone is a winner, and prizes should go to all participants.

1. Hold a contest for different types of voices, such as the scariest, sweetest or friendliest. Perhaps have contestants all say the same thing (by having a prepared script) so that sounds are based on vocal cues only.
2. Hold a contest similar to a television game show. Prizes might be awarded for the most original sounds, best vocal sound effects, or most effective vocal sounds. Parents can find winners in each category.
3. Hold an impersonation contest, using people well known to the children, such as Big Bird, Barney, one of the Wiggles, or any others the children love. If voices do not sound exactly like the character, it is okay, simply offer praise and award based on sounds, actions, originality, or most like. The point is the praise.

Applause!

Follow Me

This exercise requires good direction from the adults. I recommend that a parent or teacher demonstrate being the leader.

The leader says, "Follow me." He or she can clap hands, stomp feet, reach to the sky, and lean down to touch the floor. The actions should be reasonable for all the participants to do with some success.

They can:

- March
- Say words using different volumes and tones
- Sway like trees or plants
- Act like animals
- Pretend to mow a lawn or wash a car

All children should have an opportunity to lead. It is good to acknowledge the good leadership and encourage the participants and audience to give lots of praise after each child has performed.

Applause!

You Must Have Been a Beautiful Baby

Have the children find pictures of themselves as babies or very young children. Help them find several for the exercise. Then have the children say what they might have been thinking or doing when the picture was taken. Ask them to pretend to do what they did when the picture was made.

You can also exchange pictures among the children and have each tell the audience what they think their friend was doing at that time. Parents can help by pretending to be the child in the picture. The children can guess what the parent is acting out from the picture. Eventually, the children can begin to do the same.

This is great fun and generates lots of creative action. It is okay for parents to lose their inhibitions in this exercise as well.

Applause!

Evening News Team

Either use real movie cameras or a shoebox is a good pretend item for TV cameras. Have the children pretend to be one of the local news, weather, or sports television news team. Have certain children or parents pretend to be the camerapersons, and have them establish signals so that the people on camera will know which camera is on them at what time. This activity helps children learn eye contact while speaking.

If the cameraperson holds up a playing card, the on-camera child should look at that camera while describing a game he or she remembers, what the weather is like today, or what the neighborhood looks like. Be creative on ideas for them to talk about.

Lots of praise is helpful for the news child because they are learning a new skill that will be beneficial in their future.

Parent participation is essential in this exercise; remember to give much praise to the child who is speaking. All children should have an opportunity to be the speaker and camera operators.

Applause!

The Eyes Have It

Children can play a variation of *Mother, May I?* in which they may take certain steps forward or backward only if they establish good eye contact. Choose whatever name you want, but I like to have the children say, "Bibby, May I?"

In order to take a step forward, players must look at Bibby and say, "Bibby, May I?" If they look at Bibby, Bibby must look back and say, "Yes," while looking at them.

If Bibby does not look at the player, then the player may not move forward; if the player does so without Bibby looking, then the player must go back to the start. A little parental or teacher support to help with rules in this game is helpful. Soon the children will know the way it works, and they can do it alone.

This is a good exercise to teach children that it is important to look directly at friends and family members when telling them something. Public speakers are most affective when they can have good eye contact with their audience or individuals in conversation.

The game is a little tricky at first, but very rewarding, and allows for discussion about the game after. Let the child go on stage to tell how the game was played.

Applause!

Emotional Charades

Take pictures of children in your playgroup with them expressing an emotion, such as surprise, fear, happiness, sleepy, bored, guilty, and as many more as you can think of. It is good to have pictures of Mom, Dad, grandparents, and siblings showing emotions as well. Put the pictures in a box. Divide the playgroup into two teams and let each team take turns having members draw from the box and act out the emotion. The card should be returned to the box when the actor is finished. It is best with most groups to look at the pictures and discuss what the emotion is beforehand to be sure that all the children have a general idea of what the emotions are. The actor must act the emotion so his or her team can guess the emotion. The team may ask any questions or say anything other than say the emotion.

Variations:

1. Voice Only: Actors are placed behind a screen. By merely counting from one to ten, they must try to get their emotion across to their team using vocal cues only.
2. Face Only: Actors kneel or stand behind a table or screen so that only the face is showing. By using only the face (no voice sounds at all), they must try to get their emotion across to their team.
3. Whole Body: Actors may use any part of their bodies except their voices to get their emotion across to their team. They may not use another person in this attempt.
4. Whole Body and Voice: Actors may use their whole bodies and voices (not words, though only the numbers one through ten) to get their emotion across to their team.

The choice of variations is up to the teacher or parent initially. After a few times, the children will take the responsibility. Have fun with this one and be sure you participate along with the children.

Applause!

Survey Data

Survey data for this book was collected using forms for students to provide personal information. Comments from students quoted in the book are actual written comments from the survey.

Read the survey to see if there is something that triggers a thought about your past or how you currently view communication for your children. The tools are for gathering information and do not provide a measurement that describe your anxieties or strengths. I have received feedback from participants who tell me the questions helped them realize something about why they do the things they do relating to public speaking.

This Information is Confidential
Please respond to the following:

Your age range: 17–20 _____, 21–25 _____, 26–30 _____, 31–35 _____, 26–40 _____, 41–45 _____, 45–50 _____, 50–60 _____, Over 60 _____

Gender: Male _____ Female _____

Race: Caucasian _____, African American _____, Hispanic _____, Asian _____, Other _____

Respond to each statement by circling the number that most closely matches your personal opinion. A circle on the number "4" signifies "no opinion."

Example: Children in our current society are less creative than we were in my generation.

Strongly Agree 1 2 3 4 5 6 7 Strongly Disagree

---

1. Children in America today are less affective speaking communicators than my generation.

   Strongly Agree 1 2 3 4 5 6 7 Strongly Disagree

2. Children are given more opportunity to communicate verbally than my generation.

   Strongly Agree 1 2 3 4 5 6 7 Strongly Disagree

3. My parents encouraged me to speak in public settings.

   Strongly Agree 1 2 3 4 5 6 7 Strongly Disagree

4. When I speak before an audience, I experience high levels of anxiety (nausea, cold hands, sweating, etc.).

   Strongly Agree 1 2 3 4 5 6 7 Strongly Disagree

5. I do not experience fear when I speak before an audience.

   Strongly Agree 1 2 3 4 5 6 7 Strongly Disagree

6. I believe my fear of speaking was influenced by:

   My parents
   Strongly agree 1 2 3 4 5 6 7 Strongly Disagree

   My peers
   Strongly agree 1 2 3 4 5 6 7 Strongly Disagree

   My teachers
   Strongly agree 1 2 3 4 5 6 7 Strongly Disagree

   Other
   Strongly agree 1 2 3 4 5 6 7 Strongly Disagree

   a. Please identify "other" source: _____

7. I believe my lack of fear of speaking was influenced by:

My parents
Strongly agree 1 2 3 4 5 6 7 Strongly Disagree

My peers
Strongly agree 1 2 3 4 5 6 7 Strongly Disagree

My teachers
Strongly agree 1 2 3 4 5 6 7 Strongly Disagree

Other
Strongly agree 1 2 3 4 5 6 7 Strongly Disagree

a. Please identify "other" source: _____

Please write comments about your fear (or lack of fear) of public speaking. Please be as specific as possible. Write specific examples that come to mind about your fear or lack of fear of speaking.

_____
_____
_____
_____
_____
_____
_____
_____
_____

Endnote

1. Gibran, Kahlil, 1927. *The Prophet.* Alfred A Knopf, New York pp 18, 19.

Author Bio

Author, educator, and national orator, Ted McIlvain has shared his message with thousands of people in over forty states and four foreign countries. His interest in helping others become confident public speakers has led him to remain active in business, religious, and academic education. Clients describe Ted as an "energetic, motivational speaker with a genuine interest in every member of his audience."

Ted serves on the Adjunct Faculty of the Department of Communication Studies at Texas Christian University in Fort Worth, Texas, is a local pastor in the United Methodist Church, and has taught public speaking skills to business leaders in major corporations and benevolent organizations. He holds a Bachelor of Arts in Speech Communication from The University of Central Florida, and a Master of Science in Communication Studies from Texas Christian University. Two sons, their wives, and six grandchildren are integral parts of Ted and Sandy's life.

Printed in Great Britain
by Amazon